Blueberry Summers

Curtiss Anderson

BOREALIS
BOOKS

Blueberry Summers

{GROWING UP AT THE LAKE}

Borealis Books is an imprint of the Minnesota Historical Society Press.

www.borealisbooks.org

The Minnesota Historical Society Press is a member
of the Association of American University Presses.

Manufactured in the United States of America

10 9 8 7 6 5 4 3 2 1

∞ The paper used in this publication meets the minimum requirements of the American National Standard for Information Sciences—Permanence for Printed Library Materials, ANSI Z39.48-1984.

International Standard Book Number
ISBN 13: 978-0-87351-608-2 (cloth)
ISBN 10: 0-87351-608-7 (cloth)

Library of Congress Cataloging-in-Publication Data

Anderson, Curtiss.
    Blueberry summers : growing up at the lake / Curtiss Anderson.
        p. cm.
    ISBN-13: 978-0-87351-608-2 (cloth : alk. paper)
    ISBN-10: 0-87351-608-7 (cloth : alk. paper)
        1. Anderson, Curtiss—Childhood and youth.
        2. Anderson, Curtiss—Family.
        3. Norwegian Americans—Minnesota—Biography.
        4. Lutherans, Norwegian—Minnesota—Biography.
        5. Scandinavian American families—Minnesota.
        6. Lakes—Minnesota.
        7. Summer—Minnesota.
        8. Vacations—Minnesota.
        9. Minnesota—Social life and customs—20th century.
        I. Title.
    F615.S2A53 2008
    977.6'053092—dc22
    [B]   2007052176

Blueberry Summers was designed and set by Laurie Kania, Duluth, Minnesota. Illustrations by Matt Kania. The text type is Clifford, designed by Akira Kobayashi. The book was printed by Maple Press, York, Pennsylvania.

{M O D S W}

ANNE,
FOR
ALL
SEASONS

{Blueberry Summers}

> *"To understand America,*
> *it is merely necessary*
> *to understand Minnesota."*
> SINCLAIR LEWIS

INTRODUCTION

I was writing an article called "Islands on My Mind," where I rounded up my favorite experiences visiting some of the most captivating islands in the world. The most memorable to me were Bali, Hong Kong, Lake Rudolf in Kenya, Corfu, Malta, Venice, and oddly enough, a simple little island in a northern Minnesota lake where I spent most of my summers "so successfully disguised as a child," in the words of James Agee.

Nancy Lindemeyer, the founding editor of *Victoria* magazine, read the article and asked if I could focus on the brief section on the Minnesota lake country. I loved the idea but I knew the article would have to be short. Those halcyon days were some time ago.

"We'll run it as a reminiscence," Nancy assured me. The article could be more anecdotal than biographical. I was thrilled that my coming-of-age journey was not over after all.

For once in my life I was grateful for having been a pack rat and a compulsive note maker all my life. I have been teased and even scolded for these rituals; still, they have only intensified as I've gotten older. (Just ask Anne—Anne Sonopol Anderson, that is, MODSW—revealed here for the first time in fifty years: My Own Dear Sweet Wife. The two of us found it amusing to reduce our pet name to an acronym, for which Anne substituted "H" for "W"—husband for wife!) In my search for material for the *Victoria* article, I came across a small red diary I maintained at the lake, a record, really, of fish caught, visitors received, picnics prepared and eaten, blueberries picked—and a secret code with private stuff that I was sure only I could decipher.

I located some short pieces I had typed on discarded onionskin using my Underwood typewriter, handed down from generation to generation, with its broken letters and *o*'s that pierced the fragile paper. Among the pieces were vignettes about Great-Aunt Ingaborg, for example, and the long hot summer when I had a broken leg.

I unearthed scrawled notes and awkward sketches in school notebooks. I had even started working on a couple of novels way beyond my reach; I just hadn't lived enough nonfiction to write about it. And then there was my one-act play, *Kaptain Kemp's Kidnapping Kase,* intended to be performed in the church basement until the ever-so Reverend Johnson found out that someone got rubbed out in it.

Family and friends who had spent time at the lake with me revealed their findings, too, with snapshots, souvenirs, and storytelling. Albums filled with Brownie box-camera photos appeared by serendipity, like a visual trip through those patiently drifting days of summer.

Perhaps the most cherished of all were the huge scrapbooks I squirreled away so securely that even I couldn't find them. But my mother did, crammed in cardboard boxes that had been stacked together with industrial-strength tape and stored out of sight for years in her sewing room.

I found envelopes stuffed with unsealed handwritten letters. Most were from Sarah—who lived across the lake—and Jackie and Pearl and others from nearby lakes, farms, and towns. I was a relentless correspondent, even with friends back home in faraway Minneapolis.

A few pages celebrated holidays and events with printed programs for the Fourth of July, Memorial Day and Labor Day, county fairs, 4-H club exhibits, food festivals, and church—and still more church activities.

I had devoted more than a few pages to the much-loved dogs I had outlived. Shep was probably as old as I was when we picked him up discarded on a back road. Their dog collars were anchored to the pages in Elmer's Glue: endearing Shep and mischievous Mickey, jumpy Nebby and persnickety Bunny. *I never met a dog I didn't like.*

Any vacant nook and cranny in the house had provided shelter for these treasures that had been frequently threatened with eviction or served with hundreds of overdue parking tickets. I felt as if I should turn myself in—or be subjected to a humiliating citizen's arrest by my own mother.

The DNA-like evidence that sealed my fate was when she checked into the stacked boxes in her sewing room. She had always assumed they contained fabric swatches, spools of thread, dress patterns, and, most important, the makings of Norwegian samplers, quilts, comforters, doilies, shawls, and hotpads. Hotpads! Hotpads! Hotpads!

Threats came hurling at me like grenades: "Your father

will hear about this latest of yours . . ." "If you don't clean out this stuff by . . ." "You never look at it anyway . . ." "Before you leave for school, I want all of this out of here . . ." "You'll find your trash in the city dump." (We actually had a couple of dead grenades in the house, along with a bayonet and a German soldier's helmet with a bullet hole in it. These were all souvenirs from World War I that my dad kept in a trunk in the attic.)

Of course, my collection remained intact exactly where it was until I returned from the navy and finished college. Then most of it accompanied me to my first job of any consequence as an editor at *Better Homes and Gardens* magazine.

Alas, I had promised Nancy Lindemeyer one page. After I had written about sixteen and was on my way to more, I thought I'd better check with her. Nancy, of course, knew that any writer has a lot more to say than he thinks he has.

She laughed and said, "Send the whole thing."

I did. She published what amounts to four or five sections of this book in a somewhat different order and a somewhat different form.

Still, I couldn't stop working on the project and was soon outlining sections, trying to get a feel for the material as a book. It wasn't easy. I had no deadline, I had no assignment to continue, and I wasn't at all sure where I was going with it.

Daniel D'Arezzo, another colleague of mine at Hearst Magazines, acted as my agent for a time, and he more than anyone championed the concept of a book on a Scandinavian clan's summer holiday in the Minnesota lake country. He saw it as a celebration of the good times and a confession of the bad—not to mention a few that edge on the slapstick.

For that reason and other sensitivities, a few names have been changed. And in at least one instance, I simply couldn't remember someone's real name and had no reference to locate it. Most of these events took place in the settings I've described, but not always in the same locations or the same chronological order. The important thing is that every tale of woe or wonder actually happened and is reported as accurately as I am capable of being, given the limitations of my memory and the concern for some of the individuals involved.

Reconstructing much of the quoted material was critical for me. Most of us can't remember the exact words used even from our most memorable conversations, except in incidents that become family classics—for better or for worse.

I depended both on my myriad form of note making and my personal insights into the *intent* of these freewheeling dialogues and expressions. Unless a person has set out to deceive himself—not unheard of—he tends to remember the thrust of his exchanges with people he cares a great deal about.

If I were to give another title to this book, it would be *Things Change*. Two events of such enormity took place early in my life that made everything else almost insignificant: the Great Depression in the 1930s and World War II in the 1940s. I was much too young to comprehend the full impact of the first, and, fortunately, still too young to take part in the second. Still, these universal calamities took me from toddler to teenager.

But forgive me if I actually think my growing up was, well, about as normal as blueberry pie.

Blueberry Summers

Blueberry Summers

Come summer I was packed off to spend those simmering days on a northern Minnesota lake, one among thousands that seemed strewn like blue confetti by the hand of God. Ours was one of three lakes that channeled into each other. We simply called it Middle Lake.

Even as these isolated lakes had been patient for a glacial eternity, it seemed to me our blueberry summers would never end. No one would really age. I would remain eight, nine, ten, or twelve, at most. The blueberry patches, as onerous and glorious as life itself, would continue to stroll along our trails, climb our hills, and saunter down our valleys.

Nature would always challenge, threaten, protect, and entertain us with its sweet and sad surprises: Things would happen that had never happened before and would never happen again.

That is the essence of wilderness and wildlife.

I started thinking about summer on our lake as early as Easter. Yes, it was our lake, not the lake. With so many lakes in the region families tended to identify them as if they owned the lakes and were their sole residents. "Where is your lake?" someone might ask.

The drive up north from Minneapolis was usually uneventful, except for the discomfort of four adults and three children packaged into a two-door, Model A Ford with storage racks on the running boards and the roof loaded down with makeshift luggage, boxes, and bags. In later years, seeing photographs of the Okies fleeing the dust storms on their way to the promised land, California, I thought about us on our way to the lake.

My father and his closest friend since childhood, Leigh Johnson, occupied the front seat, often with me—the smallest—sandwiched between them. Clara, "pleasingly plump," sat in the back behind her husband, Leigh, who was usually driving. My mother was on the passenger side of the bookends with Clara, and Leigh's daughter, Carol May, and my brother, Bobby, were encased between them.

Of course, the how-much-longer-is-it-now query was relentless on my part.

"It's about five minutes closer than the last time you asked" was one of the many huffy responses.

The only real highlight of the two-hour journey was the stop in Elk River. We would each get an enormous homemade, vanilla ice-cream cone from the soda fountain at the red-brick drugstore. The shop also served "fountain Cokes" in the classic, flared fountain glasses, with ice, a squirt of secret syrup, and then the foaming soda. Never have I ever been able to recover those wondrous flavors and never did they go down so well as in those exquisite glasses.

If we had a late start, we often stopped to have a picnic organized by Clara. As far as I knew, Clara invented picnics. They were pulled together in minutes, usually featuring Clara's potato-and-egg salad with diced-up slices of leftover ham to extend its longevity to breakfast hash, then ham-bone soup, and finally burial by my dog Shep.

One of these stops gave us a lifelong tale to tell. Leigh perched the car on a hilltop where we'd have a lovely view of a lake near Anoka, Minnesota. Within seconds, a white sky turned black and blue, battered and dark, and the lake rumbled like an ocean. The funnel that dropped from the clouds seemed without form or direction, just a billowing mass soaring in the near distance.

Seconds, not minutes, passed, and the rain and winds shook our car as if the force of nature was an enormous hand, fully capable of lifting the vehicle and tossing it into the nearby lake.

"There's not one darn thing we can do, folks," Leigh said, characteristically.

My mother repeated my father's name with mounting horror: "Oh, Otto. Oh, Otto. Oh, Otto."

She was terrified by routine thunder-and-lightning storms, even heavy rains, sometimes rushing us all down to the basement of our house in Minneapolis, where the flashes couldn't be seen. But a tornado! This was Armageddon.

Her fear swept through me like a ghost, and it was years before I overcame it. It concerned my father, and more than once he snapped at my mother: "If you keep that up, you're going to have that boy afraid of his own shadow."

I wondered if we shouldn't get out of the car and run. Then it occurred to me that this monstrous funnel would swoop down and inhale everything in its path, just like the fire-tongued dragons in the movie *One Million BC* with Victor Mature.

The famous Anoka tornado struck in 1936. Later that day we drove through the devastated little town. It was virtually flattened. Straws from haystacks pierced telephone poles. Chunks of bark were torn off the trees. Everyone had a story to tell. The sheriff was running to get to his office when he was picked up by the spinning monster and deposited intact at the jail.

The highways had few threats back then—no freeways, no traffic jams, no carjacks, no road rage—and no SUVs! But the trip could be unnerving all the same. Although Leigh held the steering wheel, my mother gripped an imaginary one in the back seat. She was certain every other car coming from the opposite direction was predestined to hit us head-on.

The occasions when Leigh announced he was about to pass another car became a sort of celebrated change of pace.

"Blow your horn!" mother shouted.

"Kaw-ooo-ga . . . kaw-ooo-ga . . . kaw-ooo-ga."

We'd all stare at the wildly rounded eyes of the occupants of the car being passed. I gritted back at the gritted teeth of the driver. Shep barked a *sotto voce* — "Woo–OO—OOF"—that grew progressively louder.

Mother tapped Leigh on the back of his neck to let him know that he was passing too far over on the left. Always accommodating, he swung back to the right. Then she hit on my copilot father: "Otto, Otto, he's going to swipe the side of that car!"

My father tried but seldom succeeded in controlling the growling circumference of his voice: "Long as you're doing the driving back there anyway—why don't we just stop along here, Leigh, and let Hilda drive from the front seat."

While my mother was fully capable of driving a car, the idea of her driving on a highway was met with gasps. Someone muttered, "Gimme a tornado."

"Daddy, I have to go!" Carol May was emphatic. Any sort of excitement easily stimulated her. And when the event evoked laughter, she could become extremely incontinent.

Carol May's familiar news was met with an equally familiar chorus of inharmonious groans.

"Dagnabit, kid!" Leigh was still a long way from getting angry. "We just passed that darned car, now they'll get ahead of us, and we'll just have to pass them again—*if* we ever catch up with them again."

"Anyone who has to go had better go now," my father warned. "Boys, do you hear? Or you'll just have to use those coffee cans."

"How about you and Leigh, Otto?" Clara giggled.

Clara was just fine. She had a deck of cards and played a game she called solitary confinement all the way.

By now my mind was occupied with a sign that read unequivocally:

DULUTH 86 MILES

7

"Criminy! Eighty-six miles! And we're not even there yet."

My brother Bob, two years older, broke his vow of silence. He *hated* these trips. "And that's not even where we're going. Geez."

"I didn't say that. What a dumb—I said—"

"Just forget what you said," my father advised. "We know what you mean."

"Bob," I said, never "Bobby" as the others did; and then I'd drag his name out: "Bo-awwww-b!"

"Whaaa-t?"

"Do you spell your name with one *o* or two?"

"Out-of-state license," he interrupted my joke, which in itself had a few miles on it.

"Where?" I challenged.

"Back there. Parked there."

"I didn't see it, so it doesn't count."

"It was from Michigan. That's one point."

By then, Bob was usually ahead of me in spotting cars from other states, mostly Iowa where they don't have any lakes. Wisconsin was only worth a half point because we sort of considered it the same place as Minnesota. Bob, of course, often won, not having all the distractions I had in my effort not to miss anything, even though there was seldom anything to miss.

Now and then Leigh came to my painfully impatient rescue, nudging me with a wink and a nod. Everyone covered their ears when they could see what was coming. Leigh first, then I joined him, singing a new verse or two of a road song that had no end:

My name is Yon Yonson,
I cum from Visconsin.
I verk in da lumberyard der,
All da peeple I meet
When dey valk down da street
Sa-ay—'Hey, whaz yo' name?'
—and I tell 'em da same-ame-ame . . .
Oh, my name is Yon Yon-son,
I cum from Vis-con-sin.
I verk in da lumber-yard der.
All da peeple I meet,
When dey valk down da street
Sa-ay—'Hey, whaz yo' name?'
—and I tell 'em da same-ame-ame . . .

Leigh was laughing too hard to sing, and I struggled to continue. *"Vell, my name is . . ."*

But my father invoked his own law: "Banned!" he shouted. "That song—*song?*—is banned, forever *banned,* in every state—east of the Mississippi."

" *. . . Yon Yonson. I come from Vis . . .*"

Seeing my father break out of his glacial silence, Clara guffawed and applauded. Mother covered her mouth, but her sleek cheekbones filled fast, and she finally released a roll of giggles. Everyone stared. Laughter didn't come easy for my mother.

Carol May just assumed we had all lost it, and Bob's eyes rolled heavenward throughout the performance. Leigh and I nodded our mutual respect as performers. But more than that it was all worth it just to see my parents enjoying themselves.

By this time my exasperated query was well overdue: "*When* are *we* gonna *get there?*"

"*We* get there?" Bob said. "*We* really don't care. You just want to know when *you're* going to be there."

"Okay, then when am *I* going to get there?"

Carol May laughed but nobody else did.

Bob said, "That's the dumbest, gaa-www-d!"

Mother snapped: "Watch your language, Bobby."

Bob leaned over to my ear. "Dumb. We are all going to get there the same time as you do. Dumb. Spelled d-u-m-b."

"No," I said, "because people in the back seat will get there two seconds later. Than we do. In the front seat."

Leigh looked down at me. "Youngster, you don't want to be pushing that one too far. That could get irritating to almost anyone."

"There's a car!" I said. "Rats! Minnesota license."

Bob said, "Oh, stop!"

"No, Leigh, don't stop." I turned to the back seat. "Do you know what the dumbest thing ever said was?"

Bob said, "All I know is *you* probably said it."

Ignoring Bob, I looked at Carol May, Clara, and my mother. "I'll give you a hint. The dumbest thing ever said was the same thing as the smartest thing ever said."

Their eyes glanced off one another. "Huh?" Carol May said.

"It was that the front seat gets there before the back seat." I smiled, a moment of triumph.

Eventually, the dreaded how-much-longer question dissolved into the insufferable, "Are we there yet?"

Sometimes I realized I asked the question because it defied my father's no-nonsense reasoning: "We're *here*. Right here. *There's where.*"

At long last, the answer was a harsh but harmonious chorus of "Yaaaassss!"

Open House

When we turned onto the dirt road that led to the old farmhouse teetering on top of the hill and reflecting in the water below, I was transcended. Was I having some sort of ethereal experience, in which I felt as if I would be sheltered from harm and embraced by harmony forever? If only for a moment, I fancied the task of picking wild blueberries, so much was my heart in that summer Shangri-la.

Then a worrisome shadow would abruptly cross my brow: the dread of Labor Day—three months away—when I would have to leave the lake to go back to school in Minneapolis. I saw my life as just shy of the weight of the world on my skinny shoulders. And I must have been at least four years old.

I wondered how these grown men could afford the luxury of spending so much time at the lake? The "luxury," of course, was being unemployed! Jobs in the city were not simply scarce; they were virtually unknown. The rumor of a job somewhere—doing almost anything—was out and around before any newspaper had a chance to run an ad. And if it did, the opening was closed before anyone had a chance to inquire.

I smugly thought that the Great Depression, as it was soon labeled, was happening exclusively in the city. It was wonderful that we could spend so much time at the lake. In the city, of course, we'd gather silently, even reverently, around the radio when President Franklin D. Roosevelt held one of his fireside chats. Almost everyone viewed him as the nation's savior, who would lead us out of the Depression with his wisdom and warmth. Until I was about five years old, I thought he had *always* been President and always would be. I certainly hoped so.

When we arrived at the lake, springing from the car and splashing into the water was a required ritual of mine. I shed my overalls, which I wore over my bathing suit in anticipation. My eyes focused on the small island directly off the center of our rickety dock, which swayed with the slightest wind and creaked with each step. "Got to put in a new dock" was always the first adult proclamation. But it wasn't until I dropped the outboard motor and it went right through the dock that we finally had to build a new one. The island was close yet challenging enough to swim to, made more so because the water even by Memorial Day hadn't warmed up from winter.

Just as memorable and even more challenging were the commands from shore announcing our responsibilities, such as unloading the car, priming the water pumps, airing the bedding, cutting back the high grass, getting the boats in the water, and checking the outbuildings. The sauna was sheltered like a beloved shrine between the woodshed and the boathouse. The sun-faded red barn, where we kept the car, still leaned slightly as if it were a little exhausted. "Hey, Leigh," my father shouted, "maybe get it fixed in the fall—more help around then." Clara never resisted commenting on the annual Big Chore List: "Leigh, oh, Otto, that'll include the dock again this year, won't it?"

There was no indoor plumbing, of course. So the two-holer outhouse in the woodshed had to be opened, aired, scrubbed, and sprayed. It attracted horseflies, which my Aunt Dora said were big enough to wear English saddles. Dora was my father's sister and younger by at least ten years, and for me she was a beloved mentor more than an aunt.

The house itself stood high on a ridge with an interminable trail of wobbly stairs leading down to the lake. Wildflowers in Easter pastels lit up the gangly grass that swept down the banks, while brazen sunflowers spiraled tough and tall enough to look me right in the eye. On a hillside near the porch, great stalks of wild rhubarb thrived like ornery ground cover.

Many years earlier the reclusive structure we inhabited was a farmhouse in an area so inland and wooded that rural electrification still hadn't arrived. We had kerosene lamps that flickered musty shadows on the walls. And the wood-burning stove in the kitchen produced the world's most glorious wild blueberry pies. The stone fireplace in the living room was large enough for me to walk into, with my white head stooped, and come out looking like the end of a chimney mop.

My hair, in fact, got a lot more attention than I ever wanted, particularly from my mother. Within any twenty-four-hour period, she would study me for a moment and exclaim with the same sigh-filled conclusion: "Isn't it too bad your sister didn't get your hair?"

I dreaded this observation as much as anything I can remember, especially since I had to suffer my childhood with nicknames like Snowball and Towhead. My brother Bob enjoyed saying my hair "looked like pee in the snow." And my sister Sue, who was actually my half sister, had long, dark-brown hair. And she seemed to be perfectly happy with it. But worse was my mother's admonition that I'd better get home before dark because "bats look to land on a white head like yours that they can see at night."

Pa, my paternal grandfather, said, culling from his vast reserve of platitudes, "Norveygans haf a lot more hair den Swedes." Pa, who had a load of hair himself, took every opportunity to put down Swedes.

"Pa" was the only name I ever heard him called, including by my grandmother, his wife. Aunt Dora, the youngest of his three daughters, said that Pa felt "Grandfather" made him seem too old for his work as a commercial artist and calligrapher. Or as my mother, who didn't much like him, said: "A sign painter."

When we'd visit Pa, he'd greet us unsmilingly and unfailingly, and say: "*Hosen gaar det*?" or "How goes it?" A question he'd answer himself: "*Det gaar som det, fare sprute*"—or something akin to: "It comes and goes in spurts." I never did know what the second half meant. My father's side was predominantly blond. There were five children. Aunt Dora, my guardian angel, remained as blond as I did without any help from a bottle. Aunt Signe, the oldest, like my father was as earnest as a potato. Her shoulders were sheltered in perpetuity by a pink wool sweater; Aunt Lil was a lovely woman, outgoing and glamorous, and always left her mark on me with her lipstick. She was tiny and her hand fluttered with rings and things. Her audacious Christmas wrappings made Santa turn red with envy. Uncle Einar ("Andy") was younger than my father and more worldly. He had that Scandinavian flush of a man who orders drinks by their brand names. Uncle Andy liked himself a lot, a feat that is one of life's earliest victories—and one that was in the LOST column for his big brother.

My mother was the youngest in the Holman family of nine children, occasionally referred to as "black *Nor-vay-gans*." Her hair was dark, almost lustrous, with waves just like my brother Bob's. Four of her siblings were born in what is now the Olympic area of Norway—Holmenkollen—thus Holman or Holmen were interchangeable as the family name. They set their sites on the northern reaches of Lake Superior in Minnesota and Wisconsin, where they joined their pioneer predecessors.

Mother's father, Osvald, born in 1846, was an astonishing fifty-one years older than mother, and her eldest brother, Christ, was twenty-eight years older. Four of her handsome brothers—Anton, Carl, Oscar, and John—dominated the Washburn City Band in their spiffy uniforms. The Holmans were all musical, including mother on the piano.

I was thrilled with my uncles and their families on the infrequent occasions when we visited them. The Holman boys! One of them owned a movie theater, where I saw one of my first "talkies," the one with Jack Holt as a fighter pilot. Another brother was the mayor; he was also known as the Town Democrat back when almost everyone was a Republican. The local haberdashery was managed by the youngest brother. And it was left to the oldest, Christ, to be cheerfully called the Town Drunk.

My mother's daughter, Sue, was far better acquainted with the Holman families than with the Andersons. She was rarely at any of Grandma Anderson's family holiday gatherings. After all, she was not my father's daughter. My often imperious grandmother was in full possession of that Scandinavian vagary of ignoring unpleasant things in hopes they'll simply go away.

Sue answered only to her nickname; her first and last names were unknown to most of us. Eventually, we learned that her given name was Sedohr, sometimes spelled "Sedore," so three cheers for simply *Sue*. Her father, my mother's first husband, wasn't even Scandinavian, as far as we knew! In the course of a lifetime of incorrigible snooping, I came across some evidence (pre-DNA) that his name was something like "Cloutier." Could he have been French? Be still my heart!

Sue was married by the time I was six or seven. It was much later before I really got to know her. And I regretted that I had not been old enough to stand up for Sue when she was not included at those Anderson fêtes.

※ ※ ※

Mother and Sue were great pals. Still Sue seldom came to the lake, by her own choosing. Clara explained, "Why would a young girl as pretty as Sue want to spend all her time stuck up here with us?"

Once at the lake, the contest changed to who would get to sleep in the screened porch facing the lake and who would be relegated to the attic. Totally lacking in seniority, even with people coming and going all summer, I was usually assigned the attic.

Secretly, though, I preferred it. The attic held more privacy and mystery, with its night sounds of loons and owls and frogs and squirrels rolling acorns on the roof and timorous cries of a wolf in the woods. Under the eave I found stacks of old stuff that I'd sort through—clothes, rubber boots, fishing gear, and a treasure trove of magazines.

Early June could still be cold, with logs blazing in the living room fireplace and jackets worn outside. I relished crawling under layers of goose-down Scandinavian comforters and looking out the triangle of the attic window to the lake, sparkling with puffy spirals as if it were exhaling. In the morning, the lake was gentle, with a trail of sunlight, reflecting what I imagined were the colors of both heaven and hell.

The attic was also my writing refuge after Aunt Dora gave me the frequently handed-down Underwood typewriter that she'd used in college. The letters and lines of type were uneven and the *o*'s punctured holes in the paper, riddling it like a BB gun by the time I finished a page.

I adored Clara and Leigh Johnson as much as I did my guardian angel. They were not my relatives but in a category

all their own. They fully embraced as a way of life the biblical adage, "It is more blessed to give than to receive."

My father and Leigh had grown up together and even played semiprofessional baseball as pitcher and catcher, respectively—a fact that might well have served as a metaphor for their relationship. Leigh and Clara initiated even the simplest contact with my parents. A telephone chat? Of course, Clara called first. Break away to see a ball game in the afternoon? Leigh's idea. The new Greer Garson movie? Ditto.

If Clara could read minds, she was the most clairvoyant about my mother's. "Hilda," she'd say, "I've made a batch of potato salad—all from the garden—that'll just go to waste if we don't have a picnic." She knew my mother cherished a picnic on the level of a festival. Clara and my mother loved each other—just as Leigh and my father did—but they just didn't particularly like each other.

For as long as I can remember there had been a wall between myself and my parents. You couldn't see it or hear it, but you could feel it was there as surely as the wall between our rooms. Leigh sensed it, and in quiet times on the lake, we talked about it. Was it my father's Norsk negativism that was so difficult for me to understand as a child? My mother's melancholy? Or was it my private pain that even my brother didn't share? Was it my self-indulgence and Bob's easy indifference?

My parents didn't seem to be aware of the transformation that occurred when I arrived at the lake. From the brooding kid in the city who preferred being locked away alone in the bathroom to the ubiquitous chatterbox at the lake who had to be restrained even by Clara and Leigh from setting the agenda for the day. Looking back, I sometimes wonder if I wasn't an awful little shit. Among other things, I was so into everyone else's business my Aunt Dora christened me Snooplock Holmes.

But I can relax about it when I think of the happiness I shared with Clara and Leigh—and, yes, they with me. I wanted to be their real son. I loved being with them. I loved their smiles and laughter, and their skills and affection. A party hadn't started until they arrived, and it was over when they left. And they worshipped the lake property almost mystically, as I did, asking only to take care of it. But I think I wanted more. I wanted it to take care of me.

Clara's Kitchen

Clara took command of opening up the house for the summer as seriously any military leader ever took on an enemy, which this frail and forlorn house surely was. We all felt mobilized and battle ready, and the old house fought back with its tittering beams and broken pumps and rusty water and uneven floors and sagging mattresses.

Clara first handed out kitchen assignments, the most frequent of which was fetching pails of water from the big pump in back of the house. The small pump in the kitchen was strictly reserved for drinking water, lemonade, coffee, and coffee, and coffee. Tea? We never heard of it.

While I wasn't big on chores, I actually liked priming the outdoor pump to witness and taste the transition from the first run of iron-flavored water to its clear, cool freshness. These peculiar flavors still linger in my mouth.

The least favorite chore was to pick wild blueberries that blanketed the sweet disorder of wilderness that engulfed us. The berries sprouted along the sides of the dirt road leading to the property, tumbled down the shallow valleys, and climbed to the tops of the hills reaching for the sun. We would not be released to swim or fish until we had filled — "to the brim"—the empty two-pound Hills Bros. Coffee cans we had been issued, not to be confused with the pee cans in the car. Even in this cluster of birches and pines, it got unbearably hot, humid, and buggy with the sun beating down relentlessly on the hilltops as we extracted one small, low-lying berry after another. I tried to love them as I picked them, but I really couldn't love them until I ate them.

Once, only once, I layered my coffee can first with leaves, then blueberries, then more leaves, and finally topped off the can with berries from a bunch of plumper ones I'd held in reserve. The plot had been carefully hatched because I knew Leigh was going fishing, and I wanted to join him. I slapped my can down on the kitchen counter well in advance of the other laborers. Clara raised her eyebrows, and I smiled as if to say, "Wow, huh?"

Normally Clara didn't attend to the berries until all the cans had been accounted for. Then she'd pour them into a huge strainer for sorting and washing. I shot through the

house for the screen porch—and freedom. But I could hear Clara all the way from the dock, "Get back here, young man, before I take you over my checkered apron!"

The sadness I felt was more for the humiliation of it all than for being caught. I asked Clara if she was *disgusted* with me. "Disgust" had become a favorite word of mine, which I had been using in various forms all day, particularly directed at the blueberries.

Clara said she was not disgusted — just disappointed. My heart sank like an anchor, but Clara quickly revived my spirit. "Well, now, we'll make ourselves a small pie out of your slim pickings"—and hastily added, "Well, more like a cobbler."

She looked out in the direction of the lake. "And I'll bet there's still time for you to catch the boat. You know how slow your old pal can be." She winked and riveted her face right down to mine till our noses touched. "And you, smarty, know darn well your old pal wouldn't leave without you."

Clara knew she'd always get a big smile out of me when she called Leigh my pal.

A variety of rules had to be followed in preparing for our fishing ventures. Those directed at me were almost all Don't Forgets: "Don't forget your life jacket." "Don't forget your worm can." "Don't forget how voices carry on the lake; no jokes about folks." "Don't forget your drop line; you left it in the sink last time." "Don't forget a coat/sweater/cap ... " always followed by, "It can get cold out there."

But the most underlined and repeated command was "Don't-forget-to-go-to-the-bathroom-before you–get–in –

the–boat." In my enthusiasm, I would sometimes ignore that admonition, which ran smack into another familiar phrase after we were well out on the lake: "We have to go back 'cause I have to go!"

On one trip, Clara's father—called "Paw"—was pulling in one small bass after another, and he roared his disapproval at having to go back to shore in his heavily accented Scandinavian diphthong: "Haf' to go ver?"

"The toilet," I whispered in his ear.

Grandpa stood up in the boat, shouting and shaking his bamboo fishing pole. "Toylet, toylet, da 'ole damed lake's a toylet."

Leigh was the meticulous lord of the lake. He was such a gentle, honorable man that he even granted justice to the fish. If he judged one to be too small, it was returned to its home, despite our grumbles. But when Leigh declared the fish on my line a keeper, I cheered until the boat rocked.

There simply was no better tasting freshwater fish than walleye. Everyone set out to find walleye. And to our dismay, walleyes seemed to be getting scarcer, even back then. Once solidly hooked, a walleye averaging two-to-five pounds was not difficult to control and pull in, unlike the more gamey and less delicately flavored northern pike. Northerns were much bigger, longer, and more agile. In fact, Leigh said they were often called "aerial acrobats." An older northern could weigh in at thirty to thirty-five pounds, whereas a trophy walleye would be ten to fifteen pounds.

And then there was the dreaded bullhead. Yipes! I hated seeing that huge dark rock head with its snarly whiskers and sharp sawtoothed spines coming out of the water. In its fierce attack on the bait, a bullhead would often swallow the hook, and as I tried to extract it from the line, its evil, cold, oily, scaleless body would wind around my hand like a snake. The bullhead's spooky ways were more ominous to me because this ugly vampire really started biting in earnest after dark. Holy collywobbles!

But they were good eating. Leigh said, "The Injuns say they're tastier than trout." Most folks just throw them back in the water when they can finally get them off the hook. A lot of fishermen lose their plugs, lines, and even their poles and rods to the dark, stubborn scavengers.

Years later I was introduced to catfish, another version of bullhead. Today the fish is considered something of a delicacy, and there are luxury restaurants that raise their own in well-kept ponds. Blackened catfish (bullhead) became the rage of New Orleans Cajun cooking. So much for that mean old hooker.

The thrill of catching a fish never left me, and I knew anything I caught would be exquisitely cooked by Clara, whose triumphs in the kitchen were cherished by everyone.

Clara fried small sunfish with their delicate bones so perfectly that the skeleton lifted away like a widow's veil. She dusted northern pike and walleye with seasoned flour and allowed them to linger in her vintage wrought-iron skillet with the timing of a Barrymore.

We consumed so much fish at the lake that Clara's Spaghetti Nights, usually Saturday, were joyfully anticipated. The sauce was made from fresh garden ingredients, including our own tomatoes and herbs. Some Scandinavians never seem to get the hang of Italian meatballs, but in a quirky sort of way, Clara's Swedish meatballs were just as memorable.

None of us had heard of pasta until my mother, the least food-conscious person in our orbit, drove to a fancied-up Italian restaurant midway between the lake and her hometown of Washburn, Wisconsin, to meet her girlfriends. Mother wanted spaghetti. She laughed when she told us that one of her friends, whose father owned the restaurant, revealed that spaghetti was the same thing as pasta. "It just costs more when you call it that," she confided. Mother explained to the rest of us that the noodles were different shapes and sizes, all with unfamiliar names ending in "ini." "The ones I had looked like snails," she said.

"Uff da," Dear Old Great-Aunt Ingaborg, a frequent visitor, visibly shuddered. For a long time, I thought "Dear Old" was her first name.

"Snails!" Leigh perked up and laughed. He and my father fought in the war in France in 1917. Leigh cautioned us, "They eat them in France, you know."

"Snails?" I shouted. "Gosh, oh fishhooks!"

"Call them *escargots* over there," Leigh said.

Aunt Dora told us that in India, a country she had always dreamed of visiting — and she eventually got there — everyone says snakes tasted just like chicken.

"Uff da fey," Great-Aunt Ingaborg growled louder than her stomach.

I could tell that Clara couldn't wait to deliver her contribution. She lowered her voice and stretched the words out: "I read in my *Collier's* magazine where in China they eat dooogs."

"Oooh-ooh, God-help-us," Aunt Ingaborg winced and quivered.

Clara was possessive about her *Collier's* magazine. I was reminded many years later when I became a magazine editor just how personal a publication can be to its readers. I recall Clara being quite adamant: "Who's got my *Collier's* magazine?" And you'd better fess up if you wanted your supper.

Clara's doughnuts, never "donuts," could have made her famous had she been willing to share her recipe with the world. Her daughter, Carol May Johnson, gave me permission to publish it.

CLARA JOHNSON'S DOUGHNUTS

Stir together, then set aside:
- 3 cups sifted flour
- 1 heaping teaspoon baking powder
- ½ teaspoon nutmeg
  - pinch of salt

Beat until light in large bowl:
- 2 eggs
- 1 cup sugar

Stir in:
- 1 cup buttermilk
- 4 tablespoons lard or shortening, melted and cooled (or vegetable oil)

Stir in flour mixture until smooth; chill slightly. Roll out ³/₈-inch thick on lightly floured board.

Cut out doughnuts with floured cutter.
Let stand 15 minutes.
Fry in deep hot fat (375°F) until browned,
    turning doughnuts once.
Drain on paper towels.

Of course, everyone wandered into Clara's kitchen just to sniff in the aromas. Her coffee was clear of grounds; she mixed it with an egg yolk before adding boiling water. Clara created plump pies that should have been patented, all with ingredients from our own natural resources. She invented Blue Boy Pie (and named it!), combining blueberries, raspberries, and blackberries. Still, my all-time favorite remains strawberry rhubarb pie. I felt good about those desolate, ugly sour stalks that grew wildly nearby with no encouragement from anyone, the outcasts of the garden.

My mother, however, was not fond of cooking and had no aptitude for it. Thus, she avoided the chore whenever she could. Occasionally, guilt overcame her better judgment, and she would make a unilateral assault on the kitchen.

On one occasion, Mother resolved to duplicate Clara's doughnuts. In an attempt to outdo her, she quietly armed herself with a plastic doughnut cutter bought at Woolworths in Minneapolis before coming to the lake. I witnessed this undertaking from the door of the kitchen. Clara fled into the lake, usually something she only did after a sauna. Mother had been assured that the plastic cutter would create perfectly rounded doughnuts with perfectly rounded holes. The demonstrator at the dime store insisted that the gadget eliminated the laborious need to roll, press, cut, and form the dough.

The dough was sticky when Mother dipped the utensil into it, and she smiled at me as she raised a circle of dough with its nicely formed hole. She held it gingerly over the hot oil, and as she released the lever, the gadget melted into the pot—right up to the handle. With a shriek, Mother dumped what was left of the tool into the pot. And joined Clara in the lake.

The Father of My Heart

Leigh had an outdoor face that seemed comfortable in any kind of weather, even Minnesota's long, mean winters when almost everyone else looked ravaged. His craggy features, with deep waves across his forehead and chiseled rivulets outlining his chin, all seemed to belong exactly where they were. And I have never seen a smile so fully occupy a man's face.

He was my father's age and my father's best friend. He was also the most treasured companion of my childhood.

Early on, I sensed that the man I admired so devotedly was something of a conversation piece as well. Among the women, the talk centered on his enduring patience and thoughtfulness, with occasional snickers about his eccentricities. Leigh was known for his distinctive manner of dress. He wore round, flat top caps that I knew as stove caps, always black with a firmly extended shiny visor. On dress-up occasions he'd wear a straw boater, the ones used in movies with scenes from the turn of the nineteenth century and seen at political conventions promoting a favorite candidate on the hatband.

Leigh had a year-round wardrobe of plaid flannel shirts,

which he wore with stretch armbands above his elbows that must have been used to shorten the sleeves at a time when there was not much variety to sizes. I was never really sure what they were intended to hold up. A clip-on black leather bow tie fit snugly at his neck, and his matching black leather shoes with crisscrossed laces on bright metal studs reached fully to his calves.

All this at times equally annoyed and amused my father, who chided his longtime friend by calling him by his last name.

"Johnson! It's 90 above out here!" My father, drenched with perspiration, his face puffed and pink from the sun, continued, "Are you going to wear gloves, too?" But Leigh had a theory about keeping the heat out, and I don't ever remember seeing him sweat.

"Uncle" Skoal, blond and handsome, was often taken to be my father's younger brother. Actually, he was just a mischievous pal of both my father's and Leigh's. But Clara eyed his shenanigans suspiciously. He'd even get Leigh's goat when he didn't throw back fish that were under the weight limit.

Most women, however, never mentioned his name without adding: "He's a nice-looking Norwegian boy." Grandma, who regarded herself as a professional judge of character, clearly gave him an edge over me, less than half his age.

"Skäl"—with an umlaut over the *a*—is commonly a Scandinavian toast, but more formal and precise than "Cheers." Specifically, "Skäl" is a drinking man's admiring salute to his companions. The word is more often written as "Skäl," but Americans are prone to spelling it "skoal."

Whatever its origins, the name now belonged to Uncle

Skoal (rhymes with "coal"). I really never knew him as anything other than that. His real name was too stuffy for his bowling team in Minneapolis. He insisted that his nickname was from his ancestral Vikings, who drank from vessels made from human skulls. Clara relished toning down his embellished tales: "They were plain old *bowls,* not skulls." But no one talked about Uncle Skoal's wooden leg; surely there was an old Viking yarn behind that, too.

Skoal came on stronger than my father in bantering Leigh. "Where do you still find shoes like that, Leigh. I thought they'd stopped making them after Lincoln was shot."

The fact was that Leigh's shoes were not easy to find. He had to drive from Columbia Heights, a suburb of northeast Minneapolis, to South St. Paul, where there was a shoemaker who made them for some religious order. Leigh just liked them because they were ankle high and had soft leather. Leigh wouldn't desert his shoemaker if another one just like him moved around the corner from his house. He gave the same devotion to his barber, who had cut his hair just so since before he was married.

Leigh knew how entertained I was when he'd step back, remove his straw hat, hold it tightly to his heart, and sing out in as fine a tenor as any barbershop quartet ever produced. Leigh did sing with a quartet. All the same, Clara could never get him to sing in church, for a very good reason. Leigh didn't go to church. A particular favorite of mine was "In the Good Old Summertime." Before our summer reached its first Friday, Leigh would have me mesmerized sufficiently to overcome my wariness about singing. I'd stretch myself taller as

Leigh would bend and break out my tentative tenor until I was capable of joining his rendition of "Down by the Old Mill Stream."

My mother told our Lutheran minister how much I enjoyed singing but that I was extremely shy about my voice. He booked me right into the Easter pageant without consulting the choir director. Mother played the piano so she practiced the number I was to perform with me. It was something like this:

> *Jewels, precious jewels,*
> *Our loved and our own.*
> *Like the stars of the morning,*
> *Their great crown adorning,*
> *They shall shine in their beauty,*
> *Our loved and our own.*

Well, *something* like that. (NOTE: I have never been able to find a trace of the song or hymn anywhere; if you do, well, just keep it to yourself.)

My costume was a blue velvet biblical robe that was really one of Grandma's decorative tablecloths wrapped around me and held together with pins. All I knew was that I was some sort of magus bearing gifts for the baby Jesus. No one really told me anything about the plot. The church looked bigger than a Ringling Brothers Circus at the Minneapolis Auditorium.

The *j* in "jewels" got stuck on the way out of my mouth. The audience tittered. The organist, Hazel Bunhild Pedersen, I noticed was waving her arms up and down. I guessed she

33

meant for me to start over. At least her lips were mouthing: "Oat-var! Oat-var! Oat-var!"

When I couldn't quite get the first complete "jewels" out, Mrs. Pedersen glared at me, stopped playing, nodded with her teeth snarling, and then began pounding away again on the beleaguered organ with her right arm swinging up after every plunge.

I shrugged my shoulders, and my velvet robe started slipping off my head. The audience giggled, then covered their mouths, but I could still hear tiny gurgles. Mrs. Pedersen, in her flowery dress and Easter hat, bounded up the church stairs and yanked my hand like a vaudeville hook, causing more of my velvet robe to slide. The audience rocked with laughter. I looked back at them long enough to wave my free hand. They liked me, thank God; otherwise I would have been humiliated.

Now and then, when Skoal could coax Leigh into singing one of the more risqué songs, Skoal would join him, much to Clara's chagrin. My dad viewed this sort of thing in one of his patented poses, with his arms tightly crossed and his face reddening. My brother Bob adopted this commanding pose when he was quite small and occasionally still resorts to it.

Dad accepted Leigh's meticulousness in everything he undertook as simply being slow. "Johnson, you sure take your own sweet time getting things done." While Skoal saw Leigh as "more of a character than the rest of us put together." But it was not lost on anyone that Skoal could have used all the character Leigh could spare.

Leigh just smiled at their tedious hits and digs, but they had a way of bruising me. I think especially because Clara and Leigh did almost everything that ever got done. Since I wanted only to emulate Leigh in everything he did, I followed his lead and learned later in my life that he was merely being thorough. This attention to detail—perfectionist—was as valuable a lesson as I have ever had in my life as a writer and an editor.

"The patience of Job" was a label Leigh lived with comfortably, even from his beloved wife, Clara. And anyone who has ever fished knows that without patience, you might as well skip rocks. Like most knowledgeable fishermen, Leigh believed in striking out for the big ones in early morning and late afternoon. We'd prepare ourselves by bathing our faces, arms, and ankles in the wildly odious citronella oil to ward off bugs. Which was more offensive, the mosquitoes or that foul-smelling guck, was a toss-up. But it was the only thing on the market at that time that was truly effective.

Not having the stamina to be a fisherman, my father joined us on short forays where we could still see the house from the lake. "Impatience" is much too timid a word to describe his inability to deal with fishing. And in spite of all his banter about Leigh's wardrobe, my father arrived at the dock wearing clothes that were easily penetrable by a Minnesota mosquito. He had no sun protection, though his skin was as vulnerable as mine.

Almost before we had our lines out, we'd hear his outraged call, "Johnson, I'm being eaten alive out here." Leigh, the picture of calm, was well protected by his eccentric costume.

35

My father's casting skills were so limited he often lost his bait—minnow, worm, or plug—before it hit the water. And throwing out a line from a ten-foot bamboo pole added the hazard of one of us being hooked in the ear.

Why did my father want to set out in the boat at all? The alternative, of course, was appalling to his sense of manhood. He'd be trapped alone in the house with the women, who'd be gathered in the kitchen to chat or play Parcheesi.

Occasionally, Leigh's enduring patience was even a trial for Clara. They differed on only a few subjects. The most frequent centered on fishing. Skoal wasn't even a close second.

One summer Clara bargained with a farmer for an old cowbell to call Leigh to come in from his fishing spot on the lake. She'd ring it like Quasimodo swinging from the tower of Notre Dame. Wherever Leigh was on the lake—and I was almost always with him—he'd raise a hand gently and acknowledge the summons from the shore. "Oh, oh, looks like supper might be ready, kid." Leigh was sure he could read the bell's signals by their vigor and velocity. "Sounds like they're just setting the table."

"Daddy! Daddy!" it was Carol May's voice from shore, reinforcing the order.

I was ready. I was always hungry, even when my mother cooked. Making gravy was one of her only triumphs in the kitchen, and Clara assigned her to gravy detail. I'd just heap it over her pot roast till it was out of sight.

* * *

Carol May continued shouting "Daddy" until she was cut off by the cowbell ringing now like a melodious cyclone.

"Aw-oh, that's her, for sure." Leigh identified the blast as a final warning from the highest authority. "Mother might just be getting a bit upset now." Clara became "Mother" occasionally, just as she called Leigh "Father" or even "Daddy" now and then.

He cupped his hands to his mouth to acknowledge the order: "Yo-yo-o-yo-o-o!"

Then he turned to me sitting by the motor. "Youngster, start her up. We'll just make one last run by those reefs. I caught a nice bass over there the other day."

It took me a while to fully understand Leigh's love of fishing. It really had little to do with catching fish—or killing fish, as it's called in more sophisticated circles. Killing anything was anathema to Leigh. No, it was simply the tranquility, the beauty, and the companionship. Fishing alone had nothing to do with isolated loneliness and everything to do with peaceful solitude.

My father never understood this, not for a moment.

While I never saw Leigh's patience break, on one occasion it might have been dented. He had established a prime picnic spot on a small, wind-sheltered island on the lake, which we called "the turnaround" because it was located just before slipping into one of the main channels that led to still other adventures.

The spot had a natural anchorage for the boat with huge rocks taking the form of steps to the island surface. Leigh and friends on the lake made a rough-cut picnic table out of birch logs and situated it under an umbrella of birch trees that clustered along the shores. A neatly framed fireplace was created out of carefully selected rocks. Sometimes we'd bring firewood, although there was usually plenty of it loosely strewn around the island.

Leigh did not regard the spot as our own. It was also there for the pleasure of friends and neighbors on the lake and strangers who came upon it. There were no signs to "Keep Off." There was only respect for the manner in which the island was maintained. Leigh made the rules for the island, and everyone seemed to honor them. The most important was to leave the island cleaner than you found it.

We always arrived early enough for a swim before lunch. Clara and Leigh's spirited and loving daughter, Carol May, who was three years older than I, was the first in the water. She was a strong and efficient swimmer, faster than any of us, which I admired tremendously. Taking short, quick strokes, she moved in the water like an outboard motor. Her frequent guest at the lake, Marianne Nyborg, was a winsome blond neighbor my age who sang like an angel. She said it for all of us: "Carol May is halfway around the island by my third stroke."

Picnics, of course, also delivered the joy of Clara's potato salad made with eggs and her lemonade, to which she added ginger ale and raspberry juice. And for sheer undiluted joy, we each got to roast our very own hot dogs on tree twigs of our very own making over the open fire.

On this particular trip, after we tied up the boat, Leigh signaled his discomfort by removing his cap and scratching his head. The expression on his face suggested a number of meanings, and they were all troubling.

He stared steadily at a huge, handsome oak tree that had probably marked this shoreline for hundreds of years. Boldly carved in depth on the trunk of the tree, as if it identified the island, was the name KEVIN. I knew a Kevin from church who was about my brother's age and he lived on the lake. Leigh's eyes clouded with anguish as he shook his head. His anger, if that's what it was, wasn't the sort that made you want to hide; it made you want to cry—or pray. I was slow to recognize it because it was so rare. Like everything about him, his anger wasn't like anyone else's.

Without a word, he pushed the boat off and turned on the motor. He looked up at his distraught crew. "You folks go ahead and eat. I'll be back as soon as I can."

We all gasped at the tree. Clara blinked her eyes. "Daddy'll be all right. He'll be back."

We ate, looking out at the lake for Leigh. But we could only hear his voice, gentle but commanding, as he circled the shores: "*Kev-innn!*"

A few days later, a boy stopped by our place. He asked for Leigh. Clara told him he'd gone into town to the all-in-one-shop, which I defined in this order—the soda fountain-pharmacy-hardware-grocery. And, of course, I was with Leigh.

The boy wanted us to have his handsome catch of three-to-four pound walleyes. He said, "Just tell Leigh that Kevin came by to say hello."

Clara told us later that she was almost speechless—"but I managed to thank him. And I gave him a kiss, too. I didn't tell him I knew who he was."

Later Leigh explained: "Oh, yes, I found that rascal, Kevin. He's really a pretty good kid. He just didn't understand why we don't do things like that."

"You know, Father," Clara said. "He cleaned all those fish for us, too. Did a beautiful job."

Leigh smiled. "Well, Kevin'll be coming over to do some fishing with us. Let me tell you: That boy knows this lake like an Indian."

I had to smile. That naughty boy Kevin had just been absorbed into the tribe.

"You know something, kid," Leigh began in his most inclusive voice. "You can go fishing every day of your life, and you'll get a few bites, catch a pickerel or two, some sunfish and, if you're lucky, a nice walleye." He leaned so close to me that I could sense his emotion, so unlike him, so

40

unlike a Svenska-Norsk fisherman. "And then once in a while something *happens* that takes you by surprise."

Leigh was taking *me* by surprise; my jaw must have dropped a half inch, taking in a heavy breath. He noticed.

"Hey, now," he tapped me. "Surprises can be wonderful, too, you know. Yah! And they can be awful. Just awful."

It was as if he were preparing me for just such a happening. He knew that.

We were fishing in the blinds not far from our most untamed shoreline. I'd never heard Leigh shout out as he did.

"*A big one*," he said. He was having such a struggle reeling in his line that his catch must have swallowed the bait and the hook.

A duck had swept out of its cover in the weeds and seized the silver-rolling bait in the water, attacking it crazily. Nature can be startling and at the same time beautiful and heartbreaking. The ducks along this shore were our friends. None of us cared to hunt. We fed the ducks every day like pets, and they'd return every year. They'd waddle up to us in an order of their own design and gum the bread from our hands.

Now a duck was entangled in Leigh's hook and line, struggling desperately to be released. It had taken the hook through the roof of its mouth. Its beak was shredding, and its neck was strangling on the line.

Leigh's controlled instructions to me began with: "Your crying's not going to help me much."

I held the bird's wings, while pressing its back on the boat seat. Leigh pulled the line in the duck's mouth taut at the same time wiggling it with a wire cutter until he could see how the hook was lodged. I cringed when he had to push deeper in order to turn the hook up and pull it out.

The bird must have been in our boat for at least an hour. Her cries were pitiful. She was bleeding as Leigh held her, looking into her mouth. "The family'll rally round her, and she'll heal her mouth in the water," he said.

Gentle, too, was the father of my heart. And he was tough and curious—and he took his own sweet time.

The Great Indoors

These northern Minnesota woodlands and waters were not unlike those of the Scandinavian countries where my parents' fathers and mothers, as well as Leigh's and Clara's, were born. The early inhabitants of Minnesota's northern lake country were generally of Swedish, Norwegian, Danish, and Finnish descent. The beloved Finns, sometimes called "Scandinavians without the guilt," were known to bless their homes with splendidly made saunas before they finished the house. In fact, the saunas were often in better condition than the houses the families lived in, which was certainly true of ours. Our sauna was a small, cedar-lined room about eight-by-ten feet. A wood-burning stove, fueled from the outdoors, heated dozens of stones piled on top of it inside the sauna. Now and then, the more rugged bathers tossed a dipper or two of cold water on the stones. The steam rose instantly, like a hot slap in the face, to the three levels of benches where our pale bodies grilled, unbasted from bottom to top—rare, medium, and well. But we were warned. A small sign written in an almost-indecipherable Scandinavian-accented English with a parenthetical translation was posted in our sauna:

> *Sit on top pench at yuu own rdisk.*
> (Sit on top bench at your own risk.)
> *Member tis, tuu muts teem kets yuu reel tissy*
> (Remember this, too much steam gets you real dizzy.)
> *If svet kets in yuu eyes, chust plink a coppla dimes.*
> (If sweat gets in your eyes, just blink a couple of times.)

Few things remain more vivid to me than running naked from the steaming broth of the sauna into the dark, after-dinner ice water of the lake, more soothing than a sleeping pill. Equally awesome is my memory of the women, who used the sauna first while it was still warming but not blistering, glimpsing their bare backsides in the moonlight as they rushed into the water. Here were reserved Scandinavian women who, to my knowledge, had never previously exposed anything but their hands and faces. And in the case of Great-Aunt Ingaborg, even these were often gloved and veiled.

For years Great-Aunt Ingaborg was missing in the shuffle of family history. But everyone seemed content to welcome her back as my mother's aunt. But even that was confusing because my mother's family was seldom represented at the lake. My mother's daughter Sue, who was my half sister, had even less standing with the Anderson clan.

But Dear Old Great-Aunt Ingaborg was Norsk to the bone. She lived by herself in a rattly old house close enough to the shores of Lake Superior to hear the sound of lapping water.

That Midwestern ocean was so vast I couldn't see the other side of it, and it was so cold that on those rare times when I tried the water I splashed right out with goose bumps that looked like old measles. Superior never warmed up; it was as frigid in August as it was in May.

Aunt Ingaborg's house was also uncomfortably close to railroad tracks. On one visit, I was sound asleep when a train came through at shuddering speed. I jumped out of bed, ran through the house in my underwear, screaming at the top of my lungs, "Tornado! Tornado! Tornado!"

Great-Aunt Ingaborg lived close enough that she began making more frequent visits to the lake. Her very presence summoned an entirely new strategy for Bob, Carol May, and me. When the word went out; "Dear Old Aunt Ingaborg will be here Saturday, so be on your best behavior," we, of course, translated "best behavior" into "creating a little mischief." But the reality is that out in the country, there just wasn't a lot of mischief to go around.

A huge elm tree stood in front of the screened porch where Aunt Ingaborg sat all day, her eyes darting sharply from tree to lake to woods. Brown bears were quite brazen about eating our raspberries, well within sight of the house. To Aunt Ingaborg's horror, or so we thought, my brother and I rushed up to the porch and screamed, "There's a big brown bear in the raspberry patch." By now Aunt Ingaborg did not even spare us a glance. And to no avail, we'd try pumping up our story: "He's eating Uncle Skoal's wooden leg!" About the best we could get out of her was an "Uff da."

Aunt Ingaborg was much older than any of us ever imagined being. Mother was sure she was more than ninety years old. She could get awfully befuddled and cranky, exclaiming "Uff da!" at almost anything she considered disagreeable. Thus, she was also our prime target for another ruse that proved to be one of our most successful since it seemed to upset *everyone* in the household. We, of course, considered these antics hilarious and fell over each other roaring with laughter. "Hilarious," in fact, had become another favorite word of mine, and I managed to apply it to anything—"We caught a hilarious perch" and "There's a hilarious duck out there." If, at the moment, I thoroughly disliked someone, he would carry the burden of being called a "toad."

The attic provided more props for our antics. I found a record called "Three Little Maids from Paris" (pronounced "pair-ree"), which was considered "off-color" by the resident censor. The infamous record was not only forbidden but hidden as well. And always accessible. I never understood why the adults couldn't successfully hide the record from us or just destroy it. Perhaps they enjoyed hearing it occasionally themselves.

When no one was looking, we'd snatch the record, crank up the old phonograph, and dash off to close cover where we could hear the reaction of our elders to the shocking lyrics: "Three little maids from Pair-ree, anxious to see all that there is to see."

As I remember, some sailors were chasing these three maidens, and they all ended up at the Eiffel Tower drinking something called "une tasse de café," which I decided must be the dirty part.

The biggest blunder adults made around us was whispering, which only encouraged us to make an even greater effort to find out what was being said. When my parents spoke in a normal tone of voice, I didn't pay any attention to them. But I could pick up a mumble from forty feet: "Leigh's taking the ladies for a ride in the boat," which meant I was not included.

Although I was exasperatingly self-sufficient at the age of seven or eight, on occasion a so-called sitter was required, especially when several children were in the house. The sitter was told to take preemptive actions to discourage any disorderly shenanigans like rough-housing, "dirty" language, food fights, after-dark swimming or boating or fishing, unruly dart throwing, betting games, and movie spoofs.

I was a particular threat on doctor-patient plots with my grunting impersonation of Lionel Barrymore as Dr. Gillespie: "Now . . . see . . . here'aw, Dr. Kildare." The dummy-ventriloquist act was finally ruled out because it led to ugly exchanges over who would be my dummy.

No one in the command center of the house ever saw the truth that a far greater threat to our stability was the sitter herself. She was a large woman—a very large woman—named Naomi. Aunt Dora called her "the Bay of Naomi." She couldn't have been Norwegian because my grandfather Pa said: "Norwegians are never fat."

Naomi was thirty years old. Skoal figured she'd taken on about ten pounds a year. She broke a chair in the kitchen when she pulled it up to the icebox like it was a drive-in. And she cracked a toilet seat in the outhouse.

Naomi worked at a bakery in a nearby farm town no bigger than two sides of one street. This town got started during the heyday of iron mining. The bakery flourished, especially selling pasties to iron miners for lunch. They were like pie dough, only a lot tougher, with a variety of fillings, such as ground meats, beans, potatoes, vegetables, apples, blueberries, peaches, whatever. A couple of pasties, maybe a nickel apiece, provided a perfectly self-contained meal. The miners didn't have to lose any time to come up from their holes in the ground to eat. The mining companies often sent the pasties down the shaft free. "Just don't send 'em down with Naomi" always got a big laugh, even without adding, "She'll bury us."

With the gradual slowdown in the mining of iron ore, the town shrunk and so did the bakery. But not Naomi. Now she ate all the leftover pasties at the end of a day. When she'd sit for us, we could always depend on a modest handout of pies, which I loved, especially the ones full of beans. Oh, yes, we all went toot-toot, especially Naomi.

Naomi always made a huge batch of fudge, too. But did we get to lick the pot? No way. Naomi slammed great globs of it into her mouth with the stir spoon. Then she'd ration those big, nutty chunks like gold pieces, cutting ours up four ways, while we watched her bulbous cheeks expanding and contracting at about four chaws a chunk.

There'd always be leftovers in Clara's icebox. Naomi savored this largesse until we were in bed. She had no qualms about knocking off my supper piece of blueberry pie that I'd been saving.

Other casualties might include the remains of Clara's wonderful New England dinner of corned beef, carrots, potatoes, and cabbage. Puddings were also great favorites, and cakes—whole or in part; Naomi was not picky. And she loved my mother's cooking: "You just don't feel like you've eaten anything." My mother liked to boil a chicken for salad, then stash it away in an unlikely container. But never successfully out of sight of Naomi's X-ray eyes. However, Naomi wasn't totally indiscriminate about what she'd eat. "Just so it's cooked," she'd advise us. If it was raw or rare, Naomi dismissed it as "unhealthy." She loved my mother's cooking " 'cause it's always cooked all the way through." On ice-box inspection the next morning, Clara was surprised but never angry. The onus was on us. "I like to see those kids eat, but all this must've made them sick."

Naomi was kind of a pal. We called her "Naom." And she did warn us in her own way: "Your folks are going to be asking how you behaved. Now I want to be able to tell 'em you were all just ladies and gentlemen."

One of my early, unpublished works was dedicated to Naomi:

"Knock-knock!"
"Who's there?"
"Na-o-mi!"
"Naomi who?"
"Na-o-mi two cents!"

A live-in resident who occupied a good deal of my time was Clara's yellow canary, Jeanette. She was named after her favorite singer, Jeanette MacDonald—who, in my opinion, was no Judy Garland. I didn't like Nelson Eddy either, even if he was Scandinavian.

I thought I was irresistibly clever to observe that Jeanette's singing was "for the birds." Jeanette's namesake was known as "The Iron Canary." I got that "inside stuff" from our nearest neighbors at the lake, the Brodeen sisters, who had a vast library of movie fan magazines, which, combined with our collection in the attic, revealed just about anything you ever wanted to know about movies and movie stars.

Jeanette and I first met when I was so small I had to stretch to reach her cage. Clara sang a lilting tune when she fed her: "Hello, Little Yellow Bird." Jeanette would chime in, in her own key. When I tried to give her a little crumb, she'd bite the hand that was trying to feed her. I figured she resented having to bend down to nibble at such a measly offering.

It upset Clara that Jeannette and I were not friends. At least the bird had the good sense to like Clara's doughnuts. So I decided on a tack to win Jeanette over for Clara's sake by feeding her broken pieces of doughnuts. I still had to stand on my toes to reach eye level with the floor of her cage, and it seemed to me that Jeanette did a lot more pooping than she did warbling. Jeanette and I never did hit it off.

Among the most popular pastimes at the lake, eating came mighty close to fishing. And we vastly overate, if only to cope with being vastly overfed. On one occasion, my brother and I reached the "I-wish-I-was-dead" stage of excessive indulgence.

Our farmer friends across the lake, the Schumachers, had

huge gardens that included every variety of melon that Minnesota's short but fruitful season allowed. Their fields were gloriously patterned with feed corn for the hogs, decorative corn for displaying, and a special variety for popping. But the golden and boldest variety of them all was for eating, drizzling with fresh farm butter, yet untainted by medical research.

These bounties were complete meals in themselves for my brother and me. He was pursuing some Guinness World Record for consuming ears of corn, while I was running neck-and-neck with cantaloupe and muskmelon. Even Clara, who felt a good appetite was God's greatest blessing, admonished us to give some attention to other basic table treats like the main course.

While Bob egged me on, nibbling his way through eight ears of corn, going for a record ten, I sliced still another smiling wedge of melon eagerly matching its expression. We were engaged in a gastronomic Olympics. Now the very words, "corn on the cob," make my brother's pulse race, and he turns as green around the gills as the cobs of the corn themselves. On a summer's drive, he averts his eyes when he passes a mellowing field of corn, less he lose his longtime favorite Orco cookies. My fate was no better. My knees turn soggy at the mere sight of melon, any kind of melon. Even more threatening, the aroma of melon, any kind of melon, drifting inexorably in my direction, gives me the collywobbles.

After supper, our evenings were usually occupied by games. "Dinner" was not a weekday word; it was reserved for late afternoon on Sundays. The gaming nights were not without still more refreshments.

Carol May took charge of producing the popcorn. Fresh field popcorn was another gastronomic revelation, just as a newly laid egg is to a store egg. The nutty kernels of corn transformed into aromatic white fluffy flakes with a flavor I have never recaptured. Great bowls of it were placed at every strategic stop in the living room. I ate it in heaping handfuls.

On the dining table were pyramids of homemade brownies and huge squares of fudge, both stuffed with walnuts. This bounty would be washed down with freshly brewed coffee, raspberry lemonade with a squirt of soda, and sometimes root beer made in Grandma Anderson's cellar.

My father's coffee, however, often had more of a sour smell than an aroma, and the only thing lemony about Uncle Skoal's lemonade was a twist. In the evenings after supper, the traffic to the outhouse increased considerably among the men. And I knew why. I found the beer stashed in the barn on one of my inspections of the grounds. Otto and Skoal would slip out of the house almost without sound or motion. When Leigh left, he'd noticeably excuse himself to the ladies only to rile Paw's quick temper, accusing Leigh of being "so dam-d polite ya givin' us avay."

Clara thoroughly disapproved of alcohol. One of her closest relatives was "in his cups" more often than not, so she limited his invitations to special occasions and holidays, and then only because she adored the rest of his family, who frequently visited on their own. He was already as pickled as the beets at one dinner where Clara had me sit next to him. She figured that I was either the least embarrassable or perhaps the most unembarrassable. One time he missed his plate with a huge serving of mashed potatoes, plopping them down on Clara's white linen tablecloth, and continued right on pouring my mother's thick brown gravy over them.

The table went silent. I looked up at Clara with a gulp stuck in my throat. Clara's eyes were closed, but I could make out the strained formation of a smile on her lips. I started laughing with both hands covering my mouth. When I knew my laughter was going to get out of control, I jumped off my chair. Clara jumped up at the same time and rushed toward the kitchen. She shrieked in a high pitch that was even out of her range.

I was just behind her, laughing so hard I couldn't keep my balance. Clara's shoulders were shaking. Dear Clara fell into one of her rare and contagious laughing jags until we both had to sit down. A few of those stoic Scandinavian faces started popping into the kitchen, making us laugh even harder. Then, one person after another fell victim, and together we were all roaring to the rafters and through the roof and into the night.

Drinking and the Depression went hand in hand. Getting drunk was comforting for the men when they didn't have anywhere to go in the morning. Clara led us to understand it was better this way. A kind of courage and outrage spills over into uncontrolled hilarity.

I learned then that laughter often is a kind of crying.

A House of Cards

Name a game; we played it. I loved charades—or The Game, as Clara called it. Each team must come up with established titles of a book, movie, or song. A player then acts out the words of the title without speaking them, and the side that guesses them in the least amount of time wins.

I always wanted to be on Dora's side; no one could touch her on book titles. And the Brodeen sisters logged in as much time going to movies as going to church. Clara, always a team captain, insisted the sisters could not be on the same side. They appealed to Game Judge Leigh, who was unanimously chosen for the post because his father had been a Hennepin County court judge in Minneapolis. But Clara took the issue to a higher authority, herself—and overruled the judge.

My father dismissed our antics as "playing a girls' game," although I suspected he might have joined in if we had kept it to a single category: baseball. My brother Bob, too, could roll off baseball stats almost as fast as I could name the Seven Dwarfs—Dopey, Grumpy, Sleepy, Sneezy, Doc, Happy, Bashful—and still can. I was also a threat on Big Ten football.

The Golden Gophers of the University of Minnesota were

the reigning power, having won the most consecutive games without a loss. And then ... and then one miserable Saturday afternoon, the losingest, lowliest Indiana beat mighty Minnesota seven to zero.

My grandma was visiting; Pa never visited anyone anywhere. Grandma was foot-stompin' angry with Halsey Hall shouting over the box: "Holy cow! Holy cow! That's it, folks. That's it. The winningest team in all of football! Our Golden Gophers. Holy cow! Can you believe it, folks? Going down to a hu-mil-i-a-ting—*mortifying* defeat—holy cow!—at the hands of the last team in the league! The *Hoosiers!* At the very bottom of the Big Ten barrel. *Holy cow!*" (Years later, baseball great Phil Rizzuto, calling New York Yankees games, adopted "holy cow" as his own.)

"Uff da, uff da, hoo-lee cows!" Grandma shouted at Hall as if his head was in the box. Then she looked over at me. I was pale and glassy-eyed.

"Now vat in de vorld is dat boy cryin' from?"

Carol May did not participate in most of our games. She'd often watch and cheer us on, making it clear when she was rooting for someone by gently rubbing her hand up and down that person's back, frequently mine: "Thatta boy, Curty." Basically she was an equal-opportunity cheerleader. She wanted everyone to win!

She adored the Brodeen sisters and rubbed both their backs at the same time. The sisters never adjusted their personalities to accommodate anyone. Franklin and Eleanor Roosevelt could have joined the game, and surely one of the sisters would say, "Don't they just fit in so well?" And that was the way they saw Carol May, too, totally unaware that she was "different."

Dora was also a magnet for Carol May, drawing her out of her room, where she spent hours alone going over popular sheet music. "Where is Carol May?" Dora asked between hugs and hellos the moment she arrived. She'd extend her hand to Carol May to bring her into the party. "Sit down, and tell me what you've been doing." Dora merited Carol May's most vigorous back rubs.

I didn't fully understand that Carol May was mentally retarded. In a way, I thought all children were retarded, just because they hadn't grown up yet, including me. The most expansive comment anyone made about her limitations in front of me was, "She's just not all there." It was so characteristic of the Scandinavian reaction to any suggestion of dysfunction within the clan. At least that made it a lot easier for Clara to overlook any concern. Carol May might be *slow* perhaps, but no matter; she'd go on to school, date, and marry, even have children. But now and then some aberrant gesture or deviant comment from Carol May released the anguish in Clara's heart and the light went out in her eyes.

Oh, yes, but Detective Snooplock was on the case, just as I was in finding out the name of my half-sister Sue's father. This trait of mine was not one that a good Norwegian family admires. Trying to connect the dots this time was like picking blueberries after a spring drought. There wasn't even a paper trail. And no one would talk. Except Carol May, who told me so unabashedly, "I had a harelip when I was born."

Carol May was born with a cleft lip and palate, creating a hole in the roof of her mouth. She was profoundly disfigured. Her upper lip extended into her nose. The bones in her cheeks and the bridge of her nose were undeveloped, giving her a flattened facial structure. Having the Stickler syndrome also increased the pressure within her eyes, causing them to bulge.

The damage and the accompanying trauma went well beyond the basic birth defects, which in themselves would not have affected the brain. Carol May was not so severely retarded that she couldn't read or write. But she would never be able to advance much beyond grade school, and even then she'd be set back several times.

Carol May and I were both mad about movies. When I was too young to know any better, she explained to me that the actors were actually in the theater standing right there behind the screen. I got quite excited until I realized that Clark Gable couldn't be behind all those screens in all those movie shows in all those countries all over the world.

I told Leigh that story. He laughed. We were out fishing, just the two of us. That's when we always talked openly, but we never talked about Carol May.

He looked at me for a long time until his smile vanished. "She's a good kid, a good sport. She had terrible problems when she was born. The doctors said some of them were in the family, inherited. Mother's brother, don't you know.

"Curt, they wouldn't let Mother see her baby for a few days. They explained all the things that had gone wrong with Carol May. Most of them we never heard of. She'd need all kind of surgery when she got a few months older—and could take it.

"Then Clara's own doctor finally said he'd take her to the special care unit, so she could see her own baby. Nurses were standing around. One of 'em said: 'She's got a face only a mother could love.'

"Well, Mother heard that. And it wasn't the last time."

Clara drew much better cards as a player than as a mother. We all admired her ability at any game of chance. And we played them all—Parcheesi, Michigan, Monopoly, poker, hearts, blackjack, gin rummy, and go to the dump, a personal favorite of mine. In any game where you had a partner, I'd try every ruse to be Clara's. But more often than not, the men were pitted against the women.

My mother didn't have much interest in the games, which set up still another barrier between her and Clara. But out of the blue, Clara might say: "Oh, come on, Marie, you always do well at hearts."

To hear Clara call my mother "Marie" instead of "Hilda" brought the room to a halt. We all knew that Mother preferred her middle name, Marie, to her first. Scandinavians are stubborn about their names and almost offended by nicknames. If your proud parents blessed you with a name like Carol May, your first name remained Carol May, *not* Carol.

Mother's campaign to get everyone to call her Marie met with scant success, so this Marie moment startled the court. In any other setting, particularly with Clara introducing Mother to someone, Clara nudged the volume up a notch. "And this is Hilda, *Hilda* Anderson!"

Clara's endurance, especially in games of chance, was a match for Leigh's at fishing. She played never-say-die seven card stud till the cows came home, left, and returned again. And she was such a wonderfully happy winner that it was difficult to get upset about losing to her, even though I was never comfortable losing. But someone had to lose, and we'd all feel better if it was Leigh because it just didn't bother him. "Losing is all part of the game, folks."

Clara also exuded such confidence that her opponents felt defeated almost from the beginning. I tried to emulate her when I was allowed to play gambling games with my Mason quart jar of pennies. To this day when I find myself at a gaming table, even on the Internet, I take on the same invincible attitude.

"Set up the table, Mabel," Leigh announced, clasping his hands together. Clara usually beat me to the task of rolling out the green felt covering over the light-oak dining table that had at least two leaves for extension. Guests were expected to play even if they claimed an exemption based on some weird religious practice. One Sunday in church Clara's own pastor railed against "the gambling den within our own congregation." No one knew who squealed, but my mother was a suspect because she had complained privately, "All Clara wants to do is play cards, cards, cards."

I'd bang my Mason quart jar of pennies on the table just loud enough to alert everyone. Uncle Skoal enjoyed shaking my jar and saying, "This kid's tougher to beat than Clara." I repeatedly reminded my elders of being dealt a royal flush: ten, jack, queen, king, and ace of hearts. Leigh framed it for me, and it remains somewhere among my souvenirs.

We always played dealer's choice in poker with a variety of bizarre variations with wild cards—deuces wild; dime store or five and tens wild; hole card wild; high-low; hatband poker; no peak five card draw, and one-eyed jacks wild.

And a game I'll never forget. As the dealer, Clara called for "five card draw with jacks or better to open," which meant a player had to have at least a pair of jacks to open or make the first bet.

I opened with three cents.

Clara asked, "How many cards, honey?"

"Three," the maximum number you could draw.

After the final bet, those still in the game turned over their cards.

I had three eights.

Skoal growled. He had two pairs, a good hand. Crossly staring at Skoal, Clara slammed down her pair of kings. Leigh dropped out and looked soulfully at me. Clara closed her eyes.

"Hey, snowball, where'r your openers?" Skoal asked, looking around the table.

By now it was clear to everyone. I had opened the jacks-or-better call with a pair of eights, which did not qualify. Of course, I drew a third eight and won.

Clara didn't call me "honey" this time. "Curt, if you'd lost,

I wouldn't say a thing. But you won, and you didn't have openers."

I was humiliated—more humiliated than when I inflated my blueberry can.

"You don't want to play that way, youngster," Leigh said.

In my wild-eyed need to win, the pair of eights just looked too good to throw away, so I opened with them. I knew what I was doing. And now I froze and didn't reach for the pot.

Under these circumstances, the rules state that the pot must be left untouched in the middle of the table as a contribution to the next game. Also, I would be kicked out of the game. With a tougher crowd of players, the kicking could be literal.

"Let Curt take this small pot," Clara declared with a wink, "and let's begin again with a clean slate."

I raised my bowed head. "I better leave."

"Oh, posh," Clara said. "We're just having fun here."

"You know, when that sort of thing happens to me," Leigh said, "I'd just leave the pot."

Of course, nothing like that would ever happen to Leigh.

I took a deep breath—and turned my head away from the table, leaving the pot for the next game. Then I decided I shouldn't be in the next round, in case I won.

Cheating is despicable. Cheating your friends is dishonorable.

On at least one other occasion I failed my mentor. I had been losing too many poker hands and was getting obstreperous, something I was prone to now and then. In fact, Pa called me "bullhead" after the mulish fish that tended to swallow the hook. I could see my jar of pennies dwindling by the inch. So I jumped up from the table in a huff, grabbed the jar, and sank into a sagging corner chair to do some world-class pouting. I quit!

Later, when I reached my attic bedroom, there, in the center of the bed, was a perfectly shaped cantaloupe. Everyone knew by now that I got the collywobbles just at the smell of melon, which had become a symbol of my "sourpuss" moods—and more precisely in this case, my *greed*.

From then on, anticipating any problem with me, Clara would simply smile and sing, "Come to me my *melon*choly, baby." It never failed to lighten for me the ancestral curse that was imperative to avoid: the melancholy of Scandinavians. Our ancestors' brooding days and nights of darkness spent near the Arctic Circle seeped into our psyches and our souls like the mist from the falls of the fjords.

In the Outhouse

Of course, the outhouse had to be located as out of sight as possible, without requiring an unreasonable trek to get there. After all, sometimes you were in a hurry. So about a million years ago, the Site Selection Committee on our property chose a highly unlikely spot for socializing, picnicking, or hiking.

In short, the outhouse was located in a dreary, dark, and desolate area, heavily wooded and attractive only to the sort of creatures I spent a good deal of my time avoiding.

Once when I was very small and someone took me by the hand to go at night, Clara asked me, "Now, a big boy like you is not afraid to go out there, are you?" I was so embarrassed. Me? Afraid? I wasn't even scared of the dark. Although I did start wearing caps when my mother told me that, after sundown, bats, having no radar, find their way around by following white hair. And don't wear yellow at picnics 'cause it'll attract bees. Clara said they'll stay away if you just put out some vinegar. Clara could write a book about that sort of stuff.

Of course, I carried a dim flashlight through the darkest part of the property, the winds pushing the shadows in the woods. I'd hear my steps and stop. In the movies, there'd always be other steps just behind you. They stopped the moment you stopped.

I'd have my hand out to pull on the big wooden handle of the outhouse door before I even reached it. I'd throw open the door, leap inside, and lock it. I wasn't about to let anyone in. I'd pretend I wasn't there. Even if they shouted. Everyone must have figured that I got my toilet training at a county fair crazy house.

Consider a kid's point of view: sitting with his pants down on one side of a two-holer outhouse where it is so dark he can't see his own hand, and a bunch of loons are hanging around making what folks call their "wild laughing hack"; then they start closing in on him with one long mournful mix of boo-haas.

It gets scary out there,
There are leaks and drafts,
The place rattles.
There's buzzing: flies, spiders, mosquitoes, and bees.
Wings are flapping!
There's a rat on the roof.
A raccoon could eat the seat out from under me.
I am so thin; what if I fell in?
A snake is slithering up the side of the hole.
Something's hooting,
Something's howling,
Something's crawling.
"Aaaaagggrrhh!"

The potential for embarrassment in a two-holer facility like ours filled me with terror. In spite of the dark, I aimed for my major undertaking to be as late at night as possible, thinking this was a safer time to go when everyone else was in bed.

My worst nightmare was that I'd find myself sitting next to Great-Aunt Ingaborg, who, the adults whispered, spent an inordinate amount of time there.

Alas, going to the outhouse was the only outdoor activity I dreaded more than picking wild blueberries. Why did I have to suffer this torment? Certainly the Queen of England did not go to the toilet. And what about Eleanor Roosevelt? And movie stars?

If I were a movie star, which was under consideration from time to time, would I be the only one who did number two? It was impossible to imagine William Powell and Myrna Loy using toilet paper. Or Garbo, for God's sake. Maybe Bette Davis, but certainly not Greer Garson.

And worst of all, on more than one occasion, I was furious with myself when it turned out to be something I could have done standing up—and closer to home.

Good Neighbors, No Fences

Wild blueberries ambled aimlessly down the path to the Brodeen sisters' tiny house. The sisters called each other all sorts of nice things but seldom used their first names. Leigh sometimes called them "the Gish sisters," not because of any resemblance to Lillian and Dorothy but because of their inseparable ways and their love of movies.

For the most part, they were loving toward each other. Oh, they could snap back under certain circumstances. They never agreed on directions, for example. Just what was the safest way to drive to church on Sunday or to a movie on Saturday almost always aroused their ire. But then everyone thought they'd really be lost if they agreed.

People took them for twins and called them "the old maids" as a term of endearment. Even I was hard-pressed to tell them apart. They wore their hair in a way that looked like identical gray nightcaps.

The sisters were probably in their late fifties, older than almost everyone except Great-Aunt Ingaborg. The subject of age was strangely avoided, but when it did come up, it seemed clear that the oldest was the one with the most authority, although the more subdued sister insisted, "Well, she's not even—she's just barely older."

I figured they were old enough to be grandmothers. But they seldom had visitors. Carol May thought the sisters were schoolteachers because they taught Sunday school.

Torsti Rikavik ran Buck's Big Bait on the lower lake; we were on the middle lake, which had wide channels to the upper and lower lakes. He did a lot of handyman work for the Brodeen sisters. He was a Finn. In less than six minutes by the clock, he could pluck out a bucket of minnows all about the size Leigh wanted.

But just who was the sisters' family? Where were they? And where had the sisters worked? What were their full names? How old were they really? Were the answers to these questions more of those things stored out of sight in another big Scandinavian closet?

To my Detective Snooplock, Dora was Dr. Watson, although anyone could see that it should have been the other way around. She asked me, "Don't you ever see mail around the house, letters with their names on the envelopes?" I didn't, but maybe I just didn't look.

Dora always wrote her full name in her own books. "Because I want them back," she said. "No one seems to think books are worth returning." She figured there must be a Brodeen family Bible like Grandma's with a dedication page somewhere in the house.

I told the sisters I needed a new verse from the Bible for

attendance at Sunday school. Instead of giving your name, you had to answer by reciting a Bible verse that you had memorized. I'd been using "Thy word is a lamp unto my feet and a light unto my path" for three straight Sundays.

Hazel Bunhild Pedersen, who played the organ and directed the pageants, also taught Sunday school. I'd had my problems with her before. She was so Swedish she was practically German. She'd holler at me: "Get some new material!"

The sisters gleefully volunteered to supply me with new Bible verses. They had hundreds of them right off the top of their heads. But I said they had to be ones I selected because they're supposed to have a special meaning for me.

A pause of great solemnity hung in the air with a silence so profound that it made their cat Alley Baba's meow sound like the MGM lion. The sisters exchanged looks of mutual inspiration. Then out of the linen closet came The Book, held piously before me like a communion offering. They set me in a chair at the dining table so they could put it right in front of me. Alley's tail was always at risk when I sat in the rocking chair.

"Now you find yourself some nice passages," Elsie urged. Esther advised: "Try the New Testament. You might look at Corinthians first." Elsie, heading for the kitchen, said: "Oatmeal cookies'll be done." "You want milk or root beer?" Esther asked. "For Heaven's sake," Elsie shot back, "*milk* if he's reading the Bible."

THE HOLY BIBLE was embossed in colossal red letters, and it was bound in indented black leather with its pages edged in gold. I knew all this stuff from Pa's sign shop.

Dedicated to the Family of
Gunnar @ Marta
RIKAVIK
Loving Parents of
Torsti • Esther • Elsie

Torsti? Torsti Rikavik! What was he doing there? I looked around for the sisters. I could hear them in the kitchen. Torsti must be their brother. But the sisters' name was Brodeen. I'd better ask Leigh. He'd know.

Oh, I could sniff the oatmeal cookies coming.

"You get started with those verses?" Esther called out.

The cookies were still so warm they'd bend over. They were colossal, a word I was beginning to like. Holding one cookie took both of my hands.

"Here now. You'll want to look in the New Testament."

Elsie's voice had a decided snap: "Esther, Sonny's supposed to find ones he likes himself."

All I really wanted was to find Leigh—and Torsti. And maybe another oatmeal cookie.

Esther leaned over till her head touched mine. She started flipping through pages to the New Testament. "Now, here we are. Look here."

We were in Corinthians.

"Here's one. One of my favorites."

"Uff da, you can be so bossy," Elsie shrugged her shoulders as she bent over from the other side.

"The unmarried woman careth for the things of the Lord, that she may be holy both in body and in spirit; the married woman careth for things of the world, how she may please her husband.' Now there you go!"

Without raising her head, Elsie looked across my face at Esther's: "Holy Beelzebub! That's no Sunday school verse for a child."

Both were talking so close to my face I could feel their breath.

"If he doesn't like it, that's fine. Just use the same old standards—Matthew, Mark, Luke, John, Psalms. Fine with me. Just trying to be original."

I practically hated Esther's Corinthians. "Well, maybe it's just a little too long. See, I have to memorize all this."

Someone get me out of here!

"I hear Shep out there. He's looking for me. Better get him." I jumped up from the table, bumping heads with both sisters, and ran for the door.

I figured Leigh would be at the bait shop because he was planning to do some late night fishing—"when the big ones bite"—with Skoal and my dad.

"'When the big ones bite' means the same thing as 'the boys' night out,'" according to Clara. "How is it you guys never catch much of anything when you go out on the lake so late?"

And worst of all, late night fishing meant I wasn't invited.

I ran all the way to the bait shop, and Shep was panting, too. Leigh smiled. "I sent Shep after you, young fella." He'd say that, and I'd believe him. He'd ruffle my hair, too. It was never combed anyway. The fact is my hair has never taken to combing and still doesn't.

"Where's Torsti?" I asked. I was relieved to hear Leigh say that he was "out back getting me some night crawlers."

Torsti was always nice enough to be glad to see me. He thought we looked alike. He had white hair, too—well, yellow. But Torsti had those Finnish eyes, ancient, and I had the big blues.

After I mentioned the family Bible, Torsti asked, "Didn't you know Esther and Elsie were my sisters? They just took on Ma's last name. Those bunnies, they didn't even want to keep their first names."

The Rikavik family lived in a Finnish settlement centered around the Iron Range towns of Hibbing and Virginia.

"Pa's family's from Finland, farmers. *Ma's* from Bergen, Norway. Hotsi totsi!" Torsti leaned toward us, looked around, and almost in a whisper said, "Some folks called that a mixed marriage."

Leigh scoffed at the notion. "I never got to know your dad. Didn't know your mom at all."

"Oh, Ma. She had a bad time. First with the TB going around. She was awful sick. Stayed sick, even worse after the twins were born. But all the time, Pa took care of Ma just fine. To the day she died."

"Twins!" I was much too loud. Leigh looked sharply at me, then to the ceiling. Torsti turned to me. "You must've known Esther and Elsie were twins?"

"I didn't even know for sure their names," I said. "Nobody tells *me* anything."

Leigh was not sympathetic. "Folks tend to think you already *know* everything."

I was glad to see Torsti and Leigh have a private smile together.

"People up there liked my dad, a good Finn in a good Finnish town," Torsti said. I could tell he felt defensive. "Pop was a hockey hero, called him 'Rika.' Cheered for him: 'Rika! Rika! Rika!' He was a good businessman—and a good church-going man."

Torsti looked down at his shoes. "There was a lot more men around the range than there was women, and they got pretty loose about things, you know—"

Leigh frowned and nodded at me. "You don't have to get into detail now, Torsti. We got a young one here."

Torsti didn't seem to know he was interrupted. "Pa got himself all stuck on the church organist—"

I could have jumped out of my shoes, if I had them on. Hazel Bunhild Pedersen? "Hazel!" I almost shouted again. "Oh-a, oh-a, not Hazel Bunhild—"

"Whoa, youngster," Leigh said, "Hazel'd be too young then, and she's still here. Haven't you noticed? Your *favorite* Sunday school teacher!"

"No, no. This'un just a wee bit of a Finnish girl named Matti," Torsti said. "Course Pa and Matti had to leave the church. Kicked out! I won't soon forget those high and mighty mucky-mucks. It was all just 'contrary to God's intention,' they said in this announcement. They even dragged an apostle in there, St. Paul, like he was the state capital or something.

"It was a dumb notice. Called it 'an unscriptural divorce.' No one knew what the hell it meant. They got the language from the big church in Minneapolis where the preachers practically dress like the pope. The church elders, *none of 'em Finns!* They had it printed in the Sunday bulletin and sent all over the range towns. Pa's name on it, too, like a wanted man. Shoulda hung it in the post office, too."

Elder Gunnar Rikavik, An Unscriptural Divorce:
  To proceed premeditatively in doing that which one knows to be contrary to God's will, with the intention of becoming contrite later, makes it impossible for faith and the Holy Spirit to remain in the heart.

"Pa just brushed his hands of the whole thing. Took Matti off with him to Finland. Never returned. Scandal. Oh, those poor girls were so ashamed. They took on our mother's name. Brodeen. Norwegian. Not even Finn."

Leigh touched Torsti's arm. "You did everything for Esther and Elsie that you could—"

"You, too. And Clara. Everybody did. We all did."

"They live nicely, comfortable, and they're happy."

"Pa's angels in their nice hideaway—" Torsti's voice broke. "I didn't need to get a wife. I got my angels."

"And, Curt," Leigh said. "Did you know how popular Esther and Elsie were? Did you know they used to sing?"

"In church?"

"Bigger than church!" Torsti was emphatic. "Chautauquas!"

Chautauquas were traveling tent shows that often approached professional levels, with favorite speakers like the ubiquitous William Jennings Bryan. Bands of the John

Philip Sousa persuasion were in great demand. Even Broadway plays made their way to these rural cultural fests.

Torsti went on to tell us that "Elsie even got paid money to sing. Operatic voice. Her showstopper was 'Ah, Sweet Mystery of Life, at Last I've Found You.' She had cards printed up."

ELSIE RIKAVIK

Mezzo Soprano

Weddings • Funerals • Banquets

I was impressed. "See. See, what I always said. Elsie's practically just like a movie star."

Torsti was almost breathless. He grabbed me by the shoulders: "And you didn't know, did you? Elsie got paid. Sometimes five dollars at chautauquas. Met the famous. Well, she was the famous!"

"Esther, too?"

"Well, yes, Esther. She runs the house. Elsie keeps it cooking. Singin', I mean? Look, little buddy. Esther could run the country. She got Elsie those jobs. She put together Elsie's programs, for a happy or sad occasion, from 'My Sweet Little Alice Blue Gown' to her showstopper 'Ah, Sweet Mystery of Life.' Covered 'em all. Esther's a manager, like our Pa. Esther's older, too, and that makes a difference."

"But—not if they're twins?"

"Oh, but Esther's about twelve minutes older than Elsie. That's a big difference with girls. Look, buddy, the truth be known. Esther can't sing much better than Alley Baba can howl at loons."

The Dolls' House

When I returned from the Brodeens, Clara always asked, "Well, how are the munchkins?"

Actually, they seemed bigger to me now that I knew they were in show business. The fact is, they were smaller than I was when I was practically nine years old and didn't even reach the five-foot notch on the inside of the barn door.

Clara called the Brodeen sisters' place "the dolls' house," but their home was a much more substantial structure than ours and immaculately maintained. It was practically wall-to-wall with furniture. Dora said the odd tables with bent legs could be antiques. The satin cushions on the davenport were souvenirs. One I really liked celebrated two small Minnesota towns with the slogan: "I Pine for You and Balsam."

Torsti had painted the walls, which were covered with framed samplers of the sisters' own creation that had something nice to say about almost everyone, especially God, cats, and Bette Davis. Watching them perform their exacting cross-stitching was what I imagined it must be like watching delicate surgery. Leigh made up the words for another favorite saying of mine: "God doesn't count the hours fishing." The sisters sewed one for Leigh. They liked him so much that sometimes they called him "sonny," too.

Almost all of the sisters' hobbies required meticulous work, like needlepoint. The two of them worked like an assembly line producing homemade pot holders and hot pads. Even I couldn't escape from a visit without being given a pad or two. Esther put together throw rugs with nothing more than her hands; when completed they were scattered all over the house. She made round ones, ovals, and squares from worn clothing, bedding, towels, and even her pa's old neckties. She said they all incorporated Scandinavian, particularly Norwegian and Finnish, colors.

Together the sisters took up such a tiny space in their tiny rooms and they moved so unimposingly that their twenty-two-pound ginger cat, Alley Baba, could roam at will. His original name was "Alley Cat" until the Brodeens saw the movie, *Ali Baba and the Forty Thieves*. They loved the story so much they renamed the cat.

Sometimes, Alley seemed to take charge of the entire property. He pranced about with such neat and steady strides that he never really upset anything—or anyone, for that matter.

Clara, who was taller and almost as wide as the sisters put together, said she always got a bit dizzy when she visited the house. "Nothing quitc like a long-tailed cat in a house full of rocking chairs," she said.

Alley Baba skillfully fished off the dock with his paws. He was a cagey hunter, too, and unidentified objects had no business getting too close to the Brodeen property. He challenged raccoons, squirrels, rabbits, chipmunks, and deer. The Brodeens said that once they caught him hissing at a brown bear that was getting too near a squirrel Alley coveted.

One exception proved to be out of Alley's control—a bald eagle. Seeing a great bald eagle was as rare as thunder behind a sunset. But there it was, full of sound and fury:

"Kleek-kik-ik-ik-ik . . . khi-kak-kah-kah . . . ka-iii-ka-hi . . ."

The sisters cried out, as if imitating the eagle. I came running down the hill.

"Look, everyone!"

The eagle, with its wingspan fully seven or eight feet, sailed with urgent majesty as if to underscore its mission.

The Brodeens saw that a kitten had strayed from the cover where its mother was feeding the pride that Alley had sired. The eagle's talons, like steel and leather, swept with the rush of a wave, embracing Alley Baba's baby, lifting it and soaring off together, almost lovingly, into some other eternity.

For the Brodeens, the lake was there to look at. No one ever saw them set a toe in the water. Depending on the weather, their principal recreation aside from the Lutheran church was to attend Saturday matinee movies, which sometimes required driving great distances—thirty or forty miles.

They were entirely indiscriminate about the movies—romance, adventure, mystery, action, comedy—but preferred Bette Davis as a category unto herself. Esther, who drove the car, liked Bette Davis "when she's meaner than a hill of red ants." Elsie leaned toward a suffering Bette "when she's dying from one of those movie star diseases."

Once in town, the sisters bought copies of every movie magazine published at the time, and there were a great many. They devoured these publications, with their covers depicting stars like Jean Harlow, who looked painted rather than photographed, probably a bit of both.

The magazines rarely made an unpleasant comment about any of the stars, except in gossip columns by Hedda Hopper and Louella Parsons, who frowned on anyone who didn't live up to their narrow codes. Newspapers were a lot meaner. Walter Winchell and Jimmie Fidler took out after Charlie Chaplin and Fatty Arbuckle for their sexual exploits. The sisters didn't share these remarks with me, but I'd find them.

The sisters delighted in outfoxing each other with a movie game of their own creation. One sister named a title like *Dark Victory*, and the other had to respond instantly with the name of another movie beginning with the first letter of the last word. In this case, the letter was *V*. Last letters like *Q, V, W, X, Y, Z* were rare in movie titles, and that was the idea. *Valley of Decision* would have been a winning answer, which now required an opponent to come up with a title starting with a *D*.

Occasionally, I was allowed in the game and eventually became rather skillful. I specialized in titles for movies released for kids' matinees on triple bills: "Chester Morris as Boston Blackie," "Peter Lorre as Mr. Motto," "Sydney Toler as Charlie Chan." Instantly, two dour faces snapped, "Uff da."

The girls got really mad sometimes and said, "You're just makin' 'em up!" They objected to titles like *Charlie Chan at the Race Track*, in the belief that if they hadn't heard of it, it didn't exist.

Esther and Elsie bravely lived year-round on the lake, even after it froze and the temperature got as low as forty degrees below zero. At least the windchill factor hadn't been invented yet. Once in a while during the winter, we'd drive up to the lake from Minneapolis to go ice fishing. We'd look in on the Brodeens to see if they were in need of anything. They'd be holed up like brown bears with a veritable inferno blazing in the stone fireplace. Alley Baba had a wonderfully knitted winter wardrobe, and he wasn't the least bit inhibited about spending a good deal of his time outdoors.

The Brodeens' old Ford was tucked away in an adjoining shed under discarded quilts and blankets and rugs with a tarpaulin latched over that. Months later, the car started after an early thaw as if it had been sitting in a sauna all winter.

They always had plenty of food since they spent a good part of autumn canning and pickling. When folks from the church were near our sheltered lake, they stopped by and offered to shop for the sisters. And Torsti was always nearby.

The Schumachers, a large farm family who lived directly across the lake from us, tended to the Brodeens' needs as well. They were generous with their gifts from the land and the lake: canned meats and vegetables, fresh fish, ice, and firewood. They skied, skated, or sledded across the frozen lake.

Young Sarah Schumacher rode a horse to carry supplies to the sisters and others in the region when they were totally snowbound. Torsti posted a sign by the bait house:

ROADS ARE NOT PASSABLE
NOT EVEN JACKASSABLE

Everyone rallied 'round in Minnesota's beautiful, unaccommodating winters. Even with vast distances between us, we remained good neighbors.

You Could Be Poor without Even Knowing It

Only a valley separated us from the Brodeens, but we were
fully a lake apart from the Schumachers. Their property, once
a productive farm, had been foreclosed even before the Great
Depression in 1929. The bank had assigned the property to
despair. The Schumachers were never quite sure how they
were able to take over this solemn lineup of rickety build-
ings that had been left vacant for years.

Although he never revealed it, Torsti's father, Gunnar
Rikavik, who the so Reverend Johnson and his church ran
out of town, acquired the property with the lakeside house
for his daughters. At the same time, he turned over the farm
across the lake "to the stranded German immigrant family."
I learned later that the document actually read "to the Jewish
immigrant family presently in government custody." As Torsti
put it, "My poppa wasn't so bad, the way people said."

These were the years when living off the fat of the land
meant precisely that. But there really wasn't enough fat to
go around. Farmers were also suffering from droughts and

crop failures. It was as if nature, too, was being regulated by the economy. Farmers couldn't get loans, and foreclosures were common.

The Schumachers were drawn to this northern Minnesota region because it resembled the dark, forested farm area they'd come from in Germany. When I first knew them, they had twelve children, ranging in age from infancy to about fourteen. They were poor without even knowing it, which was entirely possible at that time.

While our house always needed fixing up, the Schumacher house, by contrast, seemed on the verge of collapse. Today it wouldn't even be called a fixer-upper, more like a tearer-downer.

The family grew, sewed, farmed, fished, trapped, or shot practically everything they ate or owned. They made blueberry wine and vinegar. They even made their own beer. Leigh would share a slug of the foam with me, then exclaim, "Best beer I've ever put in my mouth."

The farm animals enthralled me. The closest I had come to animals were my own dogs and two pet chickens, which I named Davey and Gravey, forgetting that the latter was a nice accompaniment to a plump roaster. I was mortified when my mother, known for her gravy, revealed that to me.

The Schumachers produced virtually all the food they ate: eggs, fowl, beef, pork, and veal. And they created an astonishing variety of cheeses and sausages and breads.

I was sure that Mrs. Schumacher had invented a thick, coarse bread made with stone-ground flour that I ate fresh from the oven and that still makes my mouth water when I think about it. I've never tasted anything quite like it since—and I've searched.

In the winter, they sawed blocks of ice from the lake and stored them in the barn under layers of sawdust collected from cutting trees and chopping firewood. Even in midsummer, that ice remained frozen. Nothing was wasted. They were almost completely self-sufficient or at least self-contained.

But with twelve children, clothes were harder to come by. So here was one thing everybody in the region could contribute to this much-admired clan. Yet almost before any of us had a chance to bask in our generosity, the Schumachers would have given us a cord of wood, some smoked trout, venison, fish, a block of ice, a chicken, a slab of bacon, some homemade sausage, a dozen eggs, sour-apple strudel, a loaf of pumpernickel. Giving was like a religion to them. They never took anything without giving something in return.

The family had more boys than girls, but how many of each I can't remember. However, I do recall the frequent exclamation that they were some of the handsomest, most beautiful people anyone had ever seen. And that's something for Scandinavians to say of any other nationality.

They all seemed to have huge, deep-blue eyes with enormous pupils and long, dark lashes. Their hair was wavy and dusky brown. The oldest boy, Herb, was their benevolent ruler, and his slightly younger sister, Sarah, was the princess. Together, they were the Pied Piper for their siblings, some just toddlers.

Herb and Sarah organized the children's activities, chores,

feeding, washing, bedtime, games, and sports like surrogate parents. In fact, kids from the school and nearby farms all came to the house for the sheer glory of basking in Sarah's tender, loving care. She had the sublime authority of a good teacher and the generous heart of a big sister.

The family drew me into their enchanted realm as though I were one of them. I spent as much time with the Schumachers as I was allowed to. Whenever I crossed the lake in a canoe to see them, binoculars would be focused on me from both sides. I wasn't old enough to use the outboard motorboat on my own. It was as if I had gained twelve brothers and sisters overnight.

Not only was my time spent with them venturesome and fun, but I also learned a great deal. Still innocent in the ways of farm life, I almost went into shock when I realized at their supper table that I was eating rabbit. The Easter bunny! Later, that event was topped by being served a dark, rich, gamey meat with a wonderfully tart raspberry sauce. Yes, it was Bambi! My voice trembled until I was jolted back to normal by Sarah's giggles. I prayed then that they would never serve me my good friend, the duck.

Often I'd stay overnight with one or two of the Schumacher brothers in their huge tree house, which Herb put together with wood from a collapsed shed.

Our leader liked to lecture us, but always in a protective, big brother manner. For example, Herb made it clear that Boys Don't Cry. When Herb fell out of the tree house in his sleep, he lay on the ground with a broken arm all night rather than calling out for help. When his dad found him in the morning, Herb meant it when he said, "I didn't want to wake anyone up."

One day I screwed up my courage and asked Mrs. Schumacher right out, "Didn't Herb even cry when he was a baby?"

Mrs. Schumacher's first name was Rhea, which we never used. She was very self-conscious of her German accent. Although she smiled a great deal, she seldom said anything—and never laughed. But she laughed at my question about Herb. "Oh-my," she said, as if it was one word. "Herbert wants to have never cried. He is so brave. I think we should let it be that he has never cried."

It soon became clear to me that Sarah was the most exquisitely created human being who ever lived. My only problem was that her interest in horses far exceeded any possible attraction she might have for me. Herb said, "Sarah loves kids almost as much as she loves horses." But he was always generous in advising me about Sarah. "You have to show her how much you like horses." Whoosh! I had never been able to get on a horse without a ladder.

The first time I tried to mount a horse in front of Sarah turned out to be an incredibly humiliating experience. I decided the trick was to pull myself up with all the force I could muster—which I did—but my momentum was such that I just kept going and fell off the other side.

Herb tried to encourage me with a big teasing grin. "Well, at least you're about the only boy Sarah has liked who isn't a horse."

That inspired me to confront Sarah, who was sitting

loftily astride her steed. "Sarah, don't you like people, too?"

"I like people," Sarah said, shaking back her velvety black hair, "who like horses."

There were times when I'd look at Sarah and swear she could *will* the color of her eyes to change from softly shining violet to densely plum. But it wasn't just her eyes. Dora found the word I was looking for—exotic. Sarah was sweetness itself—"the girl next door"—but in the breath of the moment she'd extend her body until her chin almost rested on her horse's head. Then she was someone else. Dora said, "She looked Eurasian." I had never heard the word before.

At that, her head disappeared into the dark mane of her mare, who received a kiss before she jogged her heels into the horse's sides. My heart leapt as they charged into the woods faster than a deer in hunting season—and time froze that image in my mind forever.

I confided in Esther and Elsie how taken I was with Sarah: "Prettier than any movie star!" I said. The twins asked, "Prettier than Hedy Lamarr?" Elsie came up with the idea that I send Sarah's photograph to Metro-Goldwyn-Mayer movie studio with the suggestion that Sarah Schumacher *replace* Hedy Lamarr, who, according to the Brodeen sisters, was giving the studio a lot of trouble. Esther added that I should assure the movie moguls that "Sarah Schumacher's name could, of course, be changed."

The Brodeens read my letter before I sent it, and they noted it should be addressed to Mr. Louis B. Mayer, the head of the studio—in Culver City, not Hollywood, as I had it. "The letter will look more professional, and Mr. Mayer, the man who runs the whole kit and caboodle, might think you're a talent scout, knowing his name like that."

Mr. Mayer did respond in a letter signed "M. Kaufman for Louis B. Mayer." Mr. Kaufman enclosed a signed eight-by-ten glossy photograph of Hedy Lamarr—signed by her! And I had been trying to get her fired. I was miserable. I was nuts about Hedy Lamarr.

Though this budding romance was strictly seasonal, Sarah and I exchanged letters after Labor Day when I returned to Minneapolis for school. Of course, the relationship suffered all the flaws of your typical younger man–older woman scenario. When we met, I was about nine, and she was easily eleven, possibly as old as twelve.

Another Fine Mess

On one of my frequent treks to the Brodeens, I found the sisters glowing with smiles as they sat around their white porcelain kitchen table. The centerpiece was a freshly baked fudge cake with thick, white fondant frosting topped with a thin layer of melted bittersweet chocolate. I could never eat plain old milk chocolate again with any interest after having tasted the Brodeens' rich dark variety.

The cake, which Esther fancifully called "the Devil's Disciple," was the triumph of every fund-raising food bazaar at the church. Celebrated as if it were a person, its name was dropped at all the ladies' meetings where there was any munching going on.

Clara's Delicate Doughnuts, sometimes sugared and frosted for the occasion, were always in the running against Esther's Devil's Disciple for the Sweet Tooth Award. I always thought the Devil's Disciple was a lot better name than that dumb "Decadent" they started calling it when the church decided "Disciple" was a slam at Jesus.

The sisters also set out the movie section of the Grand

Rapids' newspaper on the kitchen table, knowing my interest in moving pictures was almost as keen as theirs. The paper was anchored on one end by their blue enamel coffeepot and the other by a baking sheet of Toll House cookies, the original chocolate chips.

Usually, when the sisters made their famous cake, they'd follow it with a batch of cookies and even blueberry pies. Baking in a wood-burning stove was extremely sensitive, and it was considered wise to take as much advantage as possible of getting the oven to just the right temperature and maintaining it. Much to my distress, the cake was inviolate. It was to be delivered to the church that day. But the cookies were there to plunder—"Just don't get yourself sick," Elsie said.

One of the sisters pointed to the newspaper and said, "Look what we've got in store for you." My mouth was already open to accommodate a cookie, and my eyes must have been a match for it. A Laurel and Hardy movie festival was running all weekend, and the Brodeens volunteered to take me.

I couldn't have been more crazed with joy than if I'd been dealt a royal flush. Stan Laurel and Oliver Hardy were the two people who could instantly erase all my cares and woes, and I relished the thought that I carried a heavy burden of both. More than once, I heard Pa talk about "dark Norvaygans"— silent, brooding, humorless. "Oh, posh," Great-Aunt Ingaborg told me when I got older and was still worrying about being moody. "Dat's Swedes he's talking 'bout," she said. "Dat's why dey put sugar in der coffee."

* * *

Esther and Elsie seemed so tiny in the front seat of their great old touring car that to someone driving behind it must have looked like an empty car perking along the road on its own. Torsti said his poppa always loaned it for the dignitaries' car that led the Fourth of July parade. I settled in the backseat, assigned to hold the cake steady so it didn't slip around and get mauled on its way to church. Every few minutes the sisters turned to look me over, perhaps with the thought that the chief threat to that cake was its bearer.

If Elsie's breath started coming any faster, I could sense that Esther must have deviated ever so slightly from our established route.

"Are we late?" Elsie asked.

"And why do you ask?" Esther said, knowing full well why she asked.

"No matter." But it did.

Elsie said, "Sonny's back there trying to steady the cake. He's having a bit of a problem with all that wind—and speed."

Esther enunciated every word: "I-am-not-driving-fast-enough-to-pass-a-slow-dog."

"Wet your finger and you can feel the wind," Elsie said, and looked kindly at me. "You alright back there, sonny?"

"Cake's fine," I said.

A serious "aah" was beginning to form as Elsie swirled her head left to right. "You supposed to turn straight up back there."

"Noo, nooo, if I did, you'd be on your way to the province of Ontario."

"Isn't that the same gas station we already passed."

"That was last week, for heaven's sake."

I could never see that it would make much difference, since we drove so slowly that I'd forget what the first Burma Shave sign said before we reached the third one.

When we finally arrived, Hazel Bunhild Pedersen was perched at the church door to receive the cake. Turning it over to her was like the Golden Gophers losing the Little Brown Jug to Michigan.

It was fun to reach Grand Rapids on Saturday where the action centered around the new movie theater as the kids waited for the matinee to start. We'd take turns stomping on the gas station hose to make the bell ring until the attendant came running out looking for a customer. It was practically hilarious.

The Brodeens knew all about Frank and Ethel Gumm in Grand Rapids, having followed their career as vaudevillians and Elsie having herself sung at chautauquas. Frank Gumm also managed the New Grand movie theater. They had three daughters; the youngest was Frances, who got her name changed to Frances Garland on stage, then to Judy when she became a movie star. Signs about her being from there were all over Grand Rapids.

The movie house was mobbed with kids and a smattering of supervising adults from the farms and other small towns within a fifty-mile radius. Esther and Elsie were always nervous about running into Iron Range people, who might know their father and remember the girls.

Most kids piled on top of each other in the front rows of the theater. I liked to sit in back where I could see over the heads that bobbed up and down in front of me like a pot of boiling water.

The most raucous episodes in a Laurel and Hardy comedy came when Stan got Ollie's goat over some mishap that left portly Oliver plumped down in a mud puddle or hanging from the side of a roof. "Another fine mess you've gotten us into, Stanley!" Ollie seethed.

Stanley, shaking his head and near tears, then came up with some totally wacky scheme to rescue Ollie that instead landed the great round Ollie-ball in even greater despair, resulting in one of Stan's classic crying jags.

I was crying, too, laughing so hard I had tears in my eyes. My legs were tucked under me when I roared forward in my seat and collided head-on with the metal top of the seat in front of me. I slid to the floor, apparently unconscious. How was I to know?

The sisters pulled me back up into my chair. I was holding the right side of my head. When I brought my hand down, Elsie screamed, "Bleeding!" And Esther shouted loud enough to overcome the laughter, whistles, roars, and applause of the kids, who had no idea what was going on in the back rows.

A man we called the manager came running down the aisle. I used to say that he was Judy Garland's father. But she was making movies by then, and the family lived in Hollywood. When I saw blood covering my hand, felt it oozing down my forehead, and saw the sisters' faces as white as mine was red, then I think I was unconscious for sure. The manager held his own handkerchief over my right eye.

Elsie shouted for "a doctor in the house!" But everyone in the house was about ten years old. And they were all torn between missing a moment of Stan and Ollie and getting a look at the towheaded kid with the bloody face. And by then I was trying to keep my left eye clear to see the movie.

The manager half carried me to the toilet, trailed by the sisters, who stopped quickly when they saw the big bold sign MEN on the door. He sat me on the counter by the sink and turned on the water. The Brodeens remained outside, fretting and frequently knocking. "How is sonny?" Boys came in and out, and a few stayed back from the featured movie to watch me.

Finally, the manager, having my injury under some control, saw that I had a gash in the vicinity of my right eyebrow that was not about to close on its own. He ushered me past the kids, who now stared with hushed attention.

Esther had the big old Ford out front. The manager sat in the back with me, pressing my wound to control the bleeding. At the same time, he gave Esther directions to the hospital. The sisters looked back at me so often that the manager said, "We're all going to end up in the hospital."

I heard talk about stitches, and Elsie almost wailing, "Oh, sonny." No one asked me, but I'd have recommended, "No stitches. Just let it heal on its own."

When it was all over and I learned that only about three stitches were sewn over my right eyebrow, I was really disappointed. With all the blood and "icky" talk, I thought the wound would be big enough to be covered with a black patch like in a pirate movie. The scar remains to this day, camouflaged by my bushy eyebrow.

I couldn't wait to return to the theater in spite of the sisters' timid protests. It was obvious they wanted to see the rest of the cavalcade of Laurel and Hardy comedies, too. The manager, flummoxed by our stamina, said there'd be no charge. The girls got his name and planned to bring him "something special" the next time they were in town.

So with the great white bandage bulging over the right side of my face, I got enough attention from the kids to be billed as an "Extra Added Attraction," as they say on the movie posters.

Clara's Clock

Leigh remained my idol, but the lake's culture was truly defined by his ample wife, Clara. She was all crinkly smiles that lit up her cornflower-blue eyes, which were framed by close-cut, blond hair. She had a well-earned face, which she lived in with such joy that it warmed everyone around her.

Clara set the pace for our activities because of her mastery of any venture she undertook, particularly cooking. In fact, I considered her girth, always encircled by a wraparound apron, a tribute to her skills in the kitchen, and my thinness a reflection of my mother's lack of them.

Leigh particularly liked to poke around in the kitchen, sometimes to Clara's dismay. "Will you please get out of my kitchen?" Clara said, always with great affection. "I'll call you if I need you. You're just in the way now—in the way."

Like any good cook, Clara tried to limit the kitchen traffic with her declaration, "This—maximum—is a two-fanny kitchen." Although she counted Carol May and me as half-fannies, largely for our skills at washing and drying dishes.

All the same, after cleaning his fish on a makeshift scrub

board by the pump just outside the kitchen door, Leigh brought them inside and slapped them down on the kitchen counter for Clara's inspection. Clara was playfully appalled by his preemptive strikes on her kitchen, his favorite place other than a boat.

Leigh sang in barbershop quartets when he was younger, and now when tempers struck, my favorite resolution was to see Leigh wrap his arms around Clara's substantial waist and waltz her about the kitchen, singing, "Casey would waltz with the strawberry blonde—and the band played on . . ." My dad and Skoal joshed him steadily about his kitchen duties. Leigh actually did do all those useful things that cooks hate doing themselves—cutting up, cleaning up, putting away. Leigh provided solutions for any household crisis. When Clara raised a whoop, such as "I get no help around the house from Hilda," my mother, quite defensibly, took the position that Clara had everything under control and clearly did not want her in the—*her*—kitchen.

Clara and Leigh were much closer to me than any relative I'd ever known. My mother would occasionally use the phrase "your aunt Clara" to impress upon me that "she is not your mother, after all." And, of course, Clara wasn't my aunt. I guess I didn't realize how sensitive my mother was to a situation like this.

First thing in the morning, I'd head for the kitchen, where Clara always greeted me with a "Good morning, honey," adding a kiss on the cheek that sometimes landed smack on my lips, nose, ear, or the top of my head.

If my mother were there, she'd look startled. Such signs

of affection were not her style. My face turned red. Affection was—well—embarrassing. The unspoken thought that ran through my mind was: You're a big boy now—you shouldn't be getting kissed all the time. Bobby was not kissing all over the place, but he was two years older.

Still, I truly wanted to live with Clara and Leigh—maybe not all the time, just most of the time. Would that be okay with them? Would they mind telling my mother?

I said "Clara and Leigh." Their names just seemed to fall in that order, not simply because of Clara's strong presence but because of Leigh's old-time gentlemanly manner. "Ladies first" was not a cliché with him, and it didn't matter if he was getting into an automobile or a lifeboat.

Clara had the kind of grace that zoftig women often do—a style, a movement, a flair. Her decorous and purposeful handwriting fascinated me. She drew her *C* with artistic loops at the top and bottom of the letter. To the extent that I could emulate it, her *C* became mine for my first name.

I always hoped that some element of Clara's joie de vivre would rub off on my mother. They were about the same age, although Hilda was much prettier and kept her weight under control. I don't think my mother liked Clara, which saddened me terribly. More than once, she confided, "So many people take Clara for my mother! It's so embarrassing." Even with that comment, I had no notion that my mother was jealous.

Clara's delight in the mere fact of being was a magnet. At parties, her vibrant laugh enveloped a room like a big hug. Her unabashed love for Leigh was another engaging trait. Sometimes she'd call him "Daddy," which raised my eyebrows until I realized for her it meant "Darling" or "Sweetheart." Their hands clasped without their even knowing it, and Clara leaned over and kissed Leigh on the cheek as spontaneously as she'd take a sip of coffee. And they were both huggers.

Leigh was a handsome man and dapper in his own way. I always suspected that my mother had a quiet crush on him that she'd never reveal. Leigh must have been a much-sought-after bachelor in his bowler and bowtie. It seemed obvious from comments Clara—and my father—made that Leigh was something of a lady's man. But the guys called Skoal a lady-killer. There was a difference. And back then neither meant the same thing they do today.

Clara had a kind of intangible glamour, the kind that can't be taught—or bought. She and Leigh were quite sexy in a cozy sort of way. Like Gable and Crawford, movie stars that had chemistry, as the billboards exclaimed. Still I could never imagine Clara and Leigh "doing it"—whatever "it" was. At the time, I wasn't absolutely sure. I had never seen my parents touch each other. Was that something to fault them for? Or was I at fault for even thinking about it?

For Clara's many skills, one she never developed or cared to was driving a car. My mother, who did, checked that off on the plus side of the ledger in her running competition with Clara. At the lake, mother was not far from where she grew up and where her daughter Sedohr (Sue) was born. This gave her a chance to see more of her own family and friends, including a sister and several brothers who still lived in the area. They were all near strangers to the Anderson side of the enclave. As Scandinavian custom decreed, no one ever explained, much less acknowledged, the closeted enmity. My guess was that the families were separated by my mother's first marriage. That was the best I could do, even with my uncanny brilliance in undercover work.

So when mother was unavailable to drive Clara to Lutheran Church on Sundays, Leigh occasionally rescued her, although nothing made him more unhappy, since the task cut into prime fishing time when all his friends were out on the lake. Leigh also loathed the Reverend Johnson and was eager to let anyone know he was no relation to him in any way whatsoever. Clara then would reluctantly ride with the Brodeens—a dreary journey because the sisters left at 7:00 AM to teach Sunday school, which started fully two hours earlier than the service at 11:00.

Since distances were so great and farmers valued their time, especially their mornings, the church had to pack a lot of activities into those Sundays—choir practice, Teen Time, sewing circles, food bazaars, weddings, Alcoholics Anonymous, and funerals.

Gas rationing during World War II also had started about then, and folks were very sparing about using their cars. Summer people like us had the challenge of saving enough gas coupons to get up to the lake and back home. Leigh and my father pooled their coupons. Skoal was good about sharing, too, siphoning gas from his own car, since Leigh was almost always our designated driver.

The Reverend Johnson, sometimes the Very Reverend

Johnson, was less than five-feet tall—"elfin," he was called. His high forehead, lined sharply in all directions, set off his thick pompadour atop a head much too large for his body. Rimless glasses were supported precariously on his brief nose. He wore a formal black cutaway jacket with tails and striped trousers in a church that butted up against a barbed-wire fence and grazing cattle.

The reverend preached that dancing ranked on a level with devil worship, gambling was like prostitution, and drinking was a sin right up there with manslaughter. In fact, the pastor's list of really popular transgressions didn't include anything that at least one of us didn't do with considerable enthusiasm. And Skoal . . . Well, Skoal did them all.

Leigh grew up the son of a well-known county judge, when being a liberal was a compliment, and he wasn't about to be lectured by a preacher who disapproved of anything that could possibly be considered pleasurable. "That little squirt'd come out against lovemaking, if he only knew how much fun it was," Leigh said to my intense interest and total bewilderment. Leigh always reasoned that about the only way to get his wife Clara out of the church habit would be to install a one-armed bandit at the lake.

The sign outside the church always promised, "Sunday Service—11:00 AM to noon." And the Reverend Johnson always posted the subject of his sermon as well. He was especially fond of telling us where we'd end up if we didn't do everything he told us to do. One of his favorites was to become ours, too: "Do you know what hell is?" The same notice appeared just under the sermon subject every Sunday:

"Come in and hear our organist." And there was the name of my nemesis: Hazel Bunhild Pedersen.

Dora spotted it first in the church listings in the paper. Then she read it to everybody. I only had to watch her expression change to understand why all the adults were holding their sides laughing. Then I thought of Hazel Bunhild Pedersen banging away on that organ, and I rolled on the floor.

Dora sent the item to the *New Yorker*, a magazine that became a kind of shrine in my attic room. Almost nothing in print within Dora's range could escape her examination. She told me, "If there's nothing else around, I'll read the label on a can of beans." Thus launching another disconcerting habit of mine.

Clara got annoyed with the Reverend Johnson when he prefaced his sermons with what she called a dumb lie. He would say, "We'll keep it short today." At which time he seemed to smile at Clara's pouting face, then proceeded to say the same things over and over again with alterations so slight no one recognized them.

Esther sat where she could nap. If Dora was visiting, she'd attend if my mother did. Dora often said of the Very Reverend Johnson, "He's the cliché Scandinavians are stuck with." She considered his manner and dress ostentatious. Among Scandinavians, the eighth deadly sin surely was *ostentation*. And some folks believed that *I* might well be a carrier, having exposed early symptoms like "showing off."

My mother let it be known that she thought the pastor was just a flirt, which was considered just another complaint. Elsie was the holdout. She liked the Reverend Johnson.

"Because she likes being the soloist in the choir," Esther said. "And the preacher isn't much taller than her."

Leigh told me his father said you had to earn honorable titles like "reverend" and certainly "very reverend." "These aren't bestowed or ordained. They're given by the people you serve, who share a special respect for you."

Of course, Clara had a big Sunday dinner to prepare. Her complaint was not just Pastor Johnson's numbing delivery; it was not getting out of there until after one o'clock in the afternoon. And she could not depend on my mother to get the meal under way.

Clara was also an on-time person. Sunday dinner was at 3:00 PM, not 2:47 or 3:08. And if you were not in from the lake on time, it was incumbent upon her to devise some penalty. Leigh and I, of course, were the most frequent offenders—and, in the same order, her most cherished companions. Leigh's penance seemed to be something that was none of my business.

"Well, honey," she'd declare her judgment to me, "today you're getting your apple pie without cheese."

A sacred Scandinavian rhyme captures the severity of this punishment:

> *Apple pie without cheese*
> *Is like a kiss without a squeeze.*

After much thought, Clara came up with a resolution to her Sunday dinner dilemma. From the Sears catalog, which we always poured over like we were reading *Tobacco Road*,

Clara ordered a huge wall clock with bold black numerals on a white face.

The clock, which cost almost three dollars—not at all cheap at that time—was a gift to the church. Clara's note to the Very Reverend Johnson recommended that the clock be hung at eye level from his pulpit precisely on the wall opposite him. Torsti delivered the clock and hung it under Clara's supervision. Leigh would have nothing to do with it, even refusing to pay for it. But we all knew Clara paid for the clock out of her poker winnings.

God's Plan

The summer of my tenth birthday was memorable for all the wrong reasons.

School was out, and we were on the eve of leaving Minneapolis for the lake. Five of my pals, no older than I, were returning from a rousing Saturday matinee movie with Errol Flynn. Flynn, in fact, had already played a dramatic role in my life. I sat through one of his films, *The Adventures of Robin Hood,* from about two o'clock in the afternoon until midnight, when I was finally fetched by the police after an all-points bulletin went out—or so I boasted. Well, at least the police were on a lookout for a skinny white-headed kid who didn't know it was after dark. We didn't have *night* in our house; we had after dark.

I was determined to witness the climactic duel between Errol Flynn and Basil Rathbone at least one more time. I wanted to be sure Robin Hood won. Our swashbuckling games were as much a part of our lives then as perhaps video games are to kids now—only we really could get hurt! Why my parents hadn't thought to search for me in one of my natural habitats was a mystery. Evidently, they didn't think that even I could sit through the same movie five times. We found places to hide during the box office break at five o'clock when the theater was cleared and the prices went up from ten cents to twenty-five. Everyone just thought we all left when the matinee was over.

Flynn's *Robin Hood* remained my favorite movie—and it would still make my top ten list. My next encounter with Robin was on a sunny afternoon when I sat through the movie only twice.

Billy, who was not a pal, was bullying everybody, especially me. In my head, I always gave him the part of the sleaziest rogue in the movie. He had a fat, red-haired head. At school, he sat in front of me and leaned his head back over my desk, scratching his hair with both hands and releasing a storm of dandruff flakes. I finally got back at him when the dandruff collected on my history map, and I was able to pour it over his peanut butter and jelly sandwich on Wonder Bread that he just put out for lunch.

Now my pals and I were emulating our screen hero on our way home, charging up one side of a hill and down the other. With our imaginary swords, we challenged the evil Sheriff of Nottingham, the key conspirator with the villainous Prince John. I saw Billy as both, having betrayed the noble brother of John, Richard the Lion-Hearted—me.

Billy tackled me, launching me into the steep street. A car hit me in flight, which I was told later may have saved my life. If I had been crushed under the wheels of a moving van—or worse, a government vehicle, which can't be sued, well—does any accident victim ever forget the first time he hears that discomforting phrase, "You were so lucky!"

The driver loosely arranged me in the back seat of his car. No one wanted him to go to any trouble, so it was pointed out that we were only a few blocks from my house. We immediately went into a family emergency session with calls to Grandma Anderson and Aunt Signe Johnson, along with neighbors, onlookers, the driver of the attack vehicle, and even the perpetrator, Billy, speaking as an eyewitness.

I seemed to be alone in believing that my right leg was shattered and could easily be plucked apart like a wishbone. Straightening it out was impossible, and in trying, my knee seemed to be facing in the wrong direction.

"Hospital? Much too young to have to go to hospital!"—not "a" hospital or "the" hospital but *hospital* as in "asylum" or "prison." Things seldom got so desperate in a Scandinavian household that the dreaded and *costly* word "hospital" was a fit subject for conversation.

When my mother went into hospital to have a goiter operation, the *h* word was never used. Nor did anyone tell me what "goiter" meant. But mother reached for her heart so often to express stress that I was sure it had something to do with an alarming word the Anderson family often exchanged: stroke!

My father had been in the World War that hadn't gotten a number yet—and he'd seen it all. He really did. He was injured, and he was gassed. Only the enemy had masks. Dad—a word that doesn't come easy for me—no doubt saved his own life by yanking a mask off the head of a dead

German soldier. He had done his time in hospital, and he was also a jock in the tradition that a good trainer with a roll of tape would have him back in the game with Winsocki in the second half.

How a police patrol car, not far ahead of an ambulance, with flashing lights and blasting sirens arrived at our house in a neighborhood that seldom saw a stray dog became a whodunit worthy of Snooplock Holmes.

But we were closing in on a decision when we learned that mother actually called a doctor, her goiter doctor, who assumed a head-on collision had been misdirected to him. He called the police. When they arrived, they called an ambulance. And Dora picked up a familiar slur from one of the cops, "Another dumb Swede!" Pa always liked to point out, "They never say 'Norwegian'!"

The siren whirred down as the ambulance pulled into the Minneapolis General Hospital's emergency entrance. A doctor was on the spot, and he seemed to know the whole story. At the sight of us, his head rotated forlornly, and his expression clearly was that of someone whose day had been ruined.

My injuries were so severe that there was talk of my never walking again without a metal leg brace, like the Frankenstein monster. I was finally released a couple of weeks into the summer, and only then with instructions that my right leg had to be elevated with a pulley holding it at a precise level. Inside my knee, needles that self-dissolved held the multifracture in place. Urgent procedures like these were often developed on the battlefield. If wars ever have any meaning, perhaps it's that they bring about an improvement, sometimes an extraordinary advance, in medical science.

My modest consolation in all this was being upgraded from the attic to the screen porch facing the lake. Protests were made, to be sure: "He's not going to get that whole porch to himself!" However, my chief supporters—Clara and my mother—formed an uneasy alliance and advised me to ignore the attacks. Not being a native member of the household, Dora served in an advisory capacity: "Be above it all."

A last-minute surge was mounted by that pigheaded rogue Skoal. "Look, Snowball's just a kid. He doesn't need all that space. My old man used to say, 'All you need is a cot and a pot and a picture of Jesus.'"

Dora's counteroffensive was inspired: "Play on the sympathy vote. A good strong limp. Some heavy breathing."

That proved to be the winning strategy. The deal was sealed; the porch was mine. Uncle Skoal ratified the terms, henceforth known as "L-PAT," the Limited Porch Accessibility Treaty, signed in the Raspberry Patch.

Oh so Scandinavian! How we cherished our timid tarfuffles. Hamlet couldn't have had better counsel than I. Of course, Shakespeare's Hamlet was one of us, and not English at all. Observing these microscopic triumphs, it became clear to me that women almost always whopped men when the issues were essentially social. Leigh just looked the other way, Skoal compromised, and Otto ran for the woods.

So there I laid interminably, pinned up and tied down in a hospital bed cage with, more often than not, my sole companion Dear Old Great-Aunt Ingaborg, who rarely left her porch rocker when she was visiting, except to go to the outhouse.

Dora left the lake that summer without telling me she was joining the WACS (Women's Army Corps). She knew we'd both cry if she did. She enlisted Great-Aunt Ingaborg to clinch the L-PAT with Skoal, conceding access rights to the lake.

Clara was about the last of my allies. "Well, honey, makes it a lot easier on me having both you and Aunt Ingaborg so much closer to the kitchen." I started to protest that I'd rather go right back up to the attic, which I had to myself. Clara dusted off her checkered apron, leaned in my face, grimacing, "And you'd have me—huffing and puffing as I am—run up and down those attic steps with your blueberry pie."

"Criminy!" I used the word Clara penalized for excessive repetition, so I had to give a penny from my poker jar to the pot. I felt like using one of the words my classmate Ella French taught us, ones she had picked up from her big brother, who went to the Catholic school. In school, Billy the bully sat in front of me and Ella sat behind me, giving us a new dirty word every day, just as our teacher gave us a new English one.

Clara said the "*eh Mule*" was coming out in me. "Young man, you are going to work yourself up into a good old Svenska-Norsk collywobble. And pretty soon that 'bullhead' name Pa gave you is going to *stick*. Now settle down, and I'll get you a doughnut. No milk. Gotta save the rest of it for supper."

The truth is I was never comfortable with Great-Aunt Ingaborg around the house. She seldom spoke, and when she did, it was often about something disagreeable—likely as not me with my cartoon leg. So, when she just happened to be looking in my direction, I felt like one of those lopsided-looking freaky vegetables displayed at the farmers' market. And when Aunt Ingaborg really bore in on her examination of me—and I caught her at it—she'd try a smile that was clearly uncomfortable on her face.

Great-Aunt Ingaborg believed that my traumatic experience was all God's plan, and I should be content "ta larn a ting a two from hit."

I just looked down and said, "A dumb accident."

"Noooo axdent." She repeated the words with her finger shaking, "No axdent!"

I wasn't sure I could understand anything that Dear Old Great-Aunt Ingaborg said, much less learn anything, particularly with her convoluted accent that was even greater than my grandfather's.

She was also thought to be getting a bit gaw-gaw, a code I had no trouble interpreting. Words like "cantankerous" and "befuddled" were already well-established. And when she said "Uff da," that signaled mild annoyance on her part. "Uff da fey!" was foot-stomping anger.

I heard almost no talk about Aunt Ingaborg having any sort of family. Not having a husband or child, a sister or brother, struck me as unthinkable. Also, how then could she possibly be my great-aunt? And if she had a family, certainly some member of it must exist who was younger than she.

Finally, one day on the porch in the tense throes of our silence, I mustered all the courage I could and blurted out the best question I could think of, which was as dumb as, "Did you know anyone my age when you were younger?"

Since my mother's side of the family clung to their furtive little secrets like lifeboats, it took enormous persistence, of which I had no shortage, to find out that Great-Aunt Ingaborg had been married, and that her husband, Nels, was dead. "Ve say when yu dead, yu dead, not passed away."

She had a daughter, too, named Tillie. Aunt Ingaborg wanted me to see her photograph so much that she had to leave the porch to get it. She always wore long, tubular dresses, heavy brown stockings, and shoes just like the nurses, only black. She seemed almost too tall for my mother's side of the family.

Her daughter, Tillie, was very pretty, I thought, theatrical. She wore a whole lot of lipstick, her hair was dark and shiny like rayon, and her clothes looked like Betty Grable's. I was impressed that the photographer's name was printed on the picture.

Aunt Ingaborg said Nels's people had crossed the Atlantic "on da poor boots, full of cut'roats and 'rooks. Most a tem from Scot'an', way back den." Was Nels Scottish, perhaps? She wasn't sure because Nels explained—she thought to please her—that a lot of Scots were just old Norwegian Vikings.

So, whether he was Norwegian was not certain either, possibly he wasn't even Scandinavian. Wow! Certainly he must at least be a Finn, since Nels was thought to be from the Iron Range, which was dominated by immigrants from Finland.

Aunt Ingaborg tended to reveal only bits and pieces of information in any conversation. When we weren't talking, she weaved from side to side in time to her rocking. At first our exchanges started abruptly and ended just the same. She never just began with small talk like, "Vell, isonit nice day, now?" No, she just started right out with the first thing that came to mind: "Ven da iron ore run out, Nels has to verk on da big lake ... "

Soon I noticed that Aunt Ingaborg was beginning to warm up to our talks. She'd catch me studying her face. She had little vertical wrinkles around her lips, and her hands looked thinner than they really were because of the brown crevices that formed tracks to her fingers.

"Yu von ta ask sumptin', vel, yus' ask. Don' yus' look."

I was staring again, and as usual my mouth was open, which Clara called "the fly catcher."

This time Aunt Ingaborg smiled. "Da fuut hurt?"

No. Not really, it didn't. It just itched. But it was a nice question. No one else asked. Sometimes it got so tiresome, I'd just want to grab the pulley and collapse the whole darn thing. Skoal would come by to yank on the contraption, singing, "The daring young man on the flying trapeze."

Before long I became Great-Aunt Ingaborg's involuntary translator. To know that someone was finally listening to her encouraged her to say more. She was often critical of the running of the household. "Dey dunt coook veel Svenska-Norsk."

Far more important to me was my own breakthrough in understanding Aunt Ingaborg's every word, gesture, innuendo, throat clearing, snort, hahrumph, and every "jada!" "nelda!" and "uff da!" I found her stories of her husband, Nels, a man no one seemed to have ever set eyes on, as hypnotic as watching the lake when a strong wind stirred the waves into whitecaps. "Adored" may be an uneasy word for my dearly combative Great-Aunt Ingaborg, but I am helpless to think of another to describe her feelings for her wayfaring husband, a man who seemed to have been a true master of all trades. I learned that Nels had been an iron miner, and then, knowing nothing about sailing, he began working the ore boats on Lake Superior and was soon piloting them.

Nels's itinerant existence was entirely acceptable to his beloved Inga, the foreshortened name "he had blessed upon me." She said, "When our cupboards got awful bare, he became a drummer. He was a man what could sell anything."

I was soon getting skilled at converting almost anything she said in my head to listenable English. She explained that Nels started out from Bemidji, went on up to the Iron Range towns in the north—Hibbing, Chisholm, Eveleth, Virginia; then to International Falls, almost into Canada, all on one ticket!

"He'd go to one town, sell his wares, catch the next train on the same line, circle, and come back down. Then he'd pick up the stops he missed on his way up. A round-tripper paying a one-way fare. Saved himself a pretty penny." I was never quite sure how Nels was able to do this but was awed by the tale.

Nels's best-selling product was candy. "The Indians loved candy. He didn't want to tell me that he sold whiskey to them, too. Against the law! Red Lake Indian Reservation was up there, or maybe it was Nett Lake. Maybe both."

The Indians shared a secret treasure with Nels—"wild rice" that grew like gold ribbons just below the surface of Lake of the Woods, and that became a delicacy that ultimately swept the north country. "Nels was a man who never lied. Told me when he was gone so long he took to an Indian maiden, name of Mausi. Maybe a Punka Indian, I think. Means 'plucking flowers'—Mausi, not Punka.

"He saw Indians had a real need. That's when he started preaching. He branched out in that, too, being so good at anything. He'd wend his way from one tent revival to another. He'd even talk at chautauquas, and you had to be *somebody* to do that! That's where he'd meet folks like William Jennings Bryan. Nels and William Jennings Bryan took crates of fruits and vegetables that had fallen off the trains to the Indians. Some of their goods didn't just fall off by themselves.

"William Jennings Bryan became president of these United States after that."

I didn't tell her otherwise.

"Everything Nels did was with me in mind. Never forget when someone loves you like that. Remember, and *listen*. That kind of love only happens once or twice in your life, and you'd better be ready for it, and love 'em back."

Beloved Inga

Soon I realized I could listen to Great-Aunt Ingaborg for hours on that porch. And when she finally got started talking, there was no stopping her, and she had more to say than the rest of the family put together.

"What in the world do you two find to gab about all day?" my mother asked. We'd get the same sort of question from almost everyone. I liked it—and I could tell my mother liked it too—because it brought attention to her own Aunt Ingaborg and moved her closer to the family circle. And even I got more respect.

Mother's theory was that I lived in my imagination—and that's why I broke my leg, fending off pirates on Central Avenue. Aunt Ingaborg sputtered mischievously, "Yah, Hilda Marie, and I live in my memories."

When Aunt Ingaborg nodded off, I'd scribble notes with zany fury in a kid's five-year diary Dora gave me to record my experience as the Front Porch Reporter. She also set me up on the porch with her old Underwood typewriter she used in college, and even then it was a hand-me-down.

I'd begin typing in battering waves of words. The folks

playing cards in the living room were rattled by the thunderous claps of the aging Underwood. I'd get shushes building up to catcalls coming from all directions.

Aunt Ingaborg had a way of slipping behind me when she went off to bed without my knowing it. Before long, she took to patting me on top of my head as she was leaving, "G'night, sonny." Then one night, she stopped by my bed, leaned way over and kissed me on the face. And that became her "good night" signature.

Great-Aunt Ingaborg was always seeing things on the lake that I'd miss. She'd point to the thick woods to the west of us or to the eastern slope leading down to the Brodeens' house. "Did you see that? Look, look over there."

If I didn't see what she did within seconds, I'd get flustered and angry with myself. And sometimes I wondered if she'd just made it up.

"A blue heron! There—by the beaver dam."

Her voice had an urgency, as if to say, "Look now, or you'll never see it again."

Her eyes were old and cloudy; mine were young and clear. I'd seen her using a magnifying glass to read a withered old Lutheran prayer book, her lips moving.

"You don't see. You don't try so hard." She was right. I just didn't see all the things she did.

Leigh looked in on us. "You folks alright? Hear the rumbles?"

We listened.

Ingaborg touched Leigh's hand. "The Indians believe the woods groan at night and the lakes swallow."

"I think we're going to have ourselves more than a groanin'," Leigh said. "Thunder drums and a lightning show. Rain won't get in here with all that canvas overhang, but I'll move you inside if you don't feel safe."

Ingaborg and I looked at each other, simultaneously shaking our heads a vigorous *no*. We both giggled, like naughty children.

Leigh whispered in my ear, "Your mother's heading for the storm cellar."

Aunt Ingaborg showed a kind of rascally delight about the oncoming storm. It might have been at that moment when I discarded my mother's fear of weather. Leigh tried to drill in me that if you can't do anything about it, do the best you can. And Dora quoted some ancient proverb (neither the Bible nor Shakespeare, thank you) that I fell in love with for the rest of my life: There is no solution; seek it lovingly.

Ingaborg sharply pointed up at the drifting colors of the sky, as if they were riding the wind down to the water, across the lake, and through the woods. "Don't you see, sonny, now, *see?* The lake is even more beautiful when it's angry with the storm and the rain?"

It came to me then that it wasn't as if more things were happening in front of her. She just had a greater need to see them while she still could. She leaned her head against mine, her long thin arm sweeping out as if to embrace the world. She said quietly, "Look for it. Listen for it."

The same doctor in Grand Rapids who sewed up my head (when Esther and Elsie weren't around, I'd tell people five stitches, not a stingy three) drove all the way to the lake to release me from my leg contraption. People in the lake country are like that. The doctor said he just grabbed a pair of used (too tall) wooden crutches for me from the stock room. Now that I was mobile again, after about three days of steady rain, I complained to Ingaborg, "We can't fish or do anything. Can't even have a wiener roast!"

She looked kind of angry, and she was—with *me*.

"You should be happy for the rain and not be getting mad about it. Lots a rain before the fall to water the forest before it goes dry."

She sounded almost hurt that I wasn't seeing the world out there the way she did. Had I already forgotten her riveting lessons in life? No, I could see the woods burning.

"No, no, Aunt Inga," I hobbled after her, feeling almost desperate. I called her "Inga" for the first time. I rambled into a tortured explanation—or maybe it was simply defensive.

"Aunt Inga, you've made me want to do everything. Everything—I wanted to kind of please you by doing something, like fishing or—oh, you know, something I wasn't able to do for a long time. And I already did a lot of looking at the rain."

Inga had an uncommon laugh, probably because we heard it so seldom. And this time it was loud enough for my mother to hear, who came running out to us. Inga squeezed my shoulders, pulling me and my crutches to her. She looked at my mother, her niece, and said, "Hilda, I think we got ourselves another Nels here."

I went outside and just about cried. I was so thrilled. Awestruck. Me! Nels!

That last summer we saw her, dear old Great-Aunt Inga-borg began drifting more frequently from her themes. But even when she repeated them, I was her insatiable listener. I was riding those railroads myself, switching tracks as fast as I could to get back on the main line, the one-way round-trip Nels had so ingeniously devised.

But Inga was meandering so much I wasn't too sure of my interpretation anymore.

"Yu 'erd a Pool Boonyon?" she sprung on me one morning. It seems that Nels experienced the same hardships as this Minnesota folk hero, one Mr. Paul Bunyan.

"Nels just kept selling right through the northern winters. Paul Bunyan out there with his blue ox, Babe. Out there together. Snowdrifts so high they were over the top of the houses. The Elk Horn Bridge disappeared not to be seen again till spring."

It may be that the Elk Horn Bridge disappeared forever, because no such bridge has ever been heard of.

"Paul would tend to his forests with Babe. Choppin' down trees where the top of 'em came to half his size. The early

people said no one else was hardy enough—" she stopped and leaned forward to confide, "between the winter of the blue snow and the spring that came up from China."

I never questioned her—but *blue snow?* So I said, "Maybe you mean Paul's ox Babe. He was supposed to be blue." In a severe whisper, she touched my ear with her lips: "Said to be so cold, the snow turned blue!"

I could feel my breath whooshing and my heart pounding.

Dear old Great-Aunt Ingaborg, who was once treated as if she were just another relic from the attic brought down to the porch like her rocking chair for the duration of her visit. By the summer of her final days, she was an indispensable part of our lives. She was no longer a visitor. She was an important part of our summer. She was a regular. She was family.

Our beloved Inga died sitting on the screen porch, facing the lake as always. My mother called me to the porch; she was crying. "You more than anyone, she'd want to see."

I looked at Inga and her wrinkles seemed to have vanished. I smiled. Her mouth was wide open, just like mine sitting at supper with my mind on Sarah Schumacher or some other unattainable goal in life. And Clara would say, "Careful, honey, you might catch a fly, with your mouth open like that."

I walked closer to her. I only had to lean over slightly to be face to face. I had never seen a dead person before, and I touched her cheek. It certainly wouldn't have crossed my mind at the time, but years later I thought that if I had to break a leg, it may have been worth it to discover this constant, endearing, and bewitching companion.

Maybe it *was* God's plan.

Speak of the Devil

Clara would never have tolerated Skoal at the lake if her parents, who helped raise him, hadn't thought of him like a son. And he was something of an uncle to Carol May, always boosting her spirits with flattering comments and amusing gifts. More than once when Skoal approached the kitchen when Clara was talking to my mother or some visitor, she hunched her shoulders and in a stage whisper said, "Speak of the devil."

Skoal's antics entertained the men, especially my father. Leigh, unruffled by much of anything, smiled and even laughed: "Ho, ho. There he goes again, the blond bomber." Leigh and my father came on almost as strong as Skoal in their banter about his "hollow leg." I didn't know why they found this so funny until I encountered Skoal swimming one day. As he came out of the lake, I realized that one of his legs was actually wooden. My penmanship teacher in school, Miss McCall, had a wooden arm, so I could relate to this instantly.

No one ever talked about Skoal having only one leg, even when it was perfectly apparent to everyone that one of his legs would be more at home supporting the dining room table. In the Scandinavian mystique, unpleasant things go away if they are unacknowledged. Basically, no one had the Right to Know that Skoal had only one leg. No one, that is, except Snooplock Holmes.

I immediately dismissed the war as a cause. Skoal was too young to have been in Leigh and Otto's war. This might have been a hard case to crack, but important clues came to light when Carol May revealed that her father had saved Skoal from losing both legs. What?

The fact is, Skoal came close to having the only flesh-and-blood leg he had left sawed off. He was cutting trees for firewood with a chainsaw in the backyard of Clara's parents' house. Skoal's recollection is that the blade must have been loose and slipped, hitting the concrete block he was using as a perch for the logs. The blade spun the saw off balance and slashed into Skoal's leg just above the knee. The cut was deep and started bleeding violently. At that time, Leigh and Clara lived next door to her folks. As soon as Leigh caught sight of the scene, he pulled a sheet off the clothesline. By then, Skoal was practically holding his leg together with his hands. Leigh, like any good fisherman, was never without a pocketknife. He ripped at the sheet until he managed to fashion a tourniquet and get the bleeding under control.

Skoal was a volunteer fireman, so Clara called a nearby suburban fire department emergency unit. Everyone agreed that Leigh had saved Skoal's last working leg—and very possibly his life as well. To this day, every time I pass a bright red firefighters' building, I still have the urge to salute.

But Skoal—he always hated hearing the story and tried to dismiss it with an offhand comment: "Leigh was a hell of a lot more scared than I was. He almost passed out."

With Snooplock and crew on the trail of the wooden leg, the case began unraveling. Soon everyone had a theory. Then I overheard Leigh telling Skoal, "From now on let's leave this trick of sawing people in half to vaudeville where it works. You've messed it up twice now."

Clara clinched the conclusion for me when she revealed that Skoal lost his first leg performing a similar task. But this time the only thing that got locked up in one of those Scandinavian closets was his chain saw equipment.

When the inherent skills of woodworking were passed out, the tribal Andersons somehow were skipped. My father happened upon a magazine article with the unambiguous title, "How to Make a Lamp." That sort of straightforward talk appealed to him, particularly the section on making lamps with miniature ship wheels that were hooked to an on-and-off chain. Yep, when you turned the wheel right, the bulb booted on, left it went off.

When he completed his pilot model, my mother found the wood carving of the wheel, both hand and machine, a bit crude. Determined to perfect his craft, he proceeded to make more of what he called his "Viking lamps" until he regarded them as shipshape.

My mother despised them. "They're a nuisance. It's easier to just pull the chain."

My father gave his Viking lamps to just about anyone who'd accept one, bulb included. I'm sure they were hustled out for display whenever he visited.

Later I upheld the family incompetence by converting my beloved early Underwood typewriter to a lamp. You'd simply press *o-n* and, of course, *o-f-f*. Viewers were not so unkind as to call my typewriter lamp a "nuisance." They more or less settled for "ridiculous."

My father and Uncle Skoal both wisely gave up woodworking as a hobby. Skoal, however, clung to his favorite pastimes, drinking and women, neither of which is acknowledged in any registry of American hobbies. Aunt Dora, who found Skoal quite attractive, said that in any accounting of his interests, "Women would finish in a dead heat with gin."

Backwoods bars in northern Minnesota lake country are institutions that merit a sociological study in themselves. Uncle Skoal would be the guide of choice for any scholar undertaking the task. Skoal's search for new bars was certainly as dogged as Leigh's for new fishing holes.

Occasionally, Leigh would suggest fishing at a nearby lake for a change of pace—and luck. After a few hours of slow fishing, Skoal smartly maneuvered the party to a "nice-looking joint I spotted a couple weeks ago."

When naming their joint, owners of backwoods bars in northern Minnesota choose from only about ten basic names. The savviest proprietor seldom runs out of fingers before he reaches "The Black Bear Bar," with its memorable history, so proclaimed by a plaque over the saloon door:

On a dark and stormy night
a great black bear
crashed through the front door
in search of food.
Among our brave patrons,
who mostly remained seated,
the Reverend Lars Vederoff
swore on his own Daddy's Bible
that the notorious "Big Black Foot"
weighed between 650 and 930 pounds.
You'll want to be here when he returns—
and they say he always does . . .
Words here were written by my own daughter,
Gusta Soderquist.

   (signed) *Knud Soderquist, Owner and Proprietor*

Leigh was reluctant to allow me to go on these bar ventures, but Skoal just propped me up on the bar, bought me an Orange Crush and some beer peanuts and gave me a few nickels to play the pinball machine. In these joints, I developed an arm for darts, too, and years later I did not embarrass America in London pubs.

I made no effort to dislike Uncle Skoal, as a few members of the clan advocated. My mother caved in with, "Just don't let him set an example for you."

Of what? I was well aware that I had a kind of risky streak that made my mother nervous. I was ready for challenges, not simple childish dares. Halloween tricks or treats were for children. I was ready for adventures, like running away from home. Outrageous behavior fascinated me as long as it didn't do anyone any harm. It must have been in the family. My brother Bob's athleticism motivated him to try just about anything.

Skoal liked having me go around to the bars with him, and the backwoods bars made no fuss about age. I proved to be an amusing distraction to other patrons, and that had to be worth something. I heard everything from "Isn't he cute?" to "Here, kid, want some nickels." Skoal paid particular attention when I was getting the towhead rub from a good-looking woman.

My favorite bar turned out to be so lost in the woods that we had to park and walk about a half mile to get to it. The bartender was a Sioux Indian. A picture over the bar depicted the Battle of Wounded Knee. Indians are now properly known as Native Americans, and the Sioux are referred to as the Dakota.

It soon became apparent why this bar was one of Skoal's favorites. He had already given the bartender a name on a previous visit—Heap, as in you-know-what. Heap rarely poured anything but shots and beer, together or separately, and, of course, had no idea what a martini was.

But Skoal wanted to give him a fair shake at it. Heap decided with good reason that the drink was composed entirely of Martini & Rossi vermouth. He proceeded to fill a tumbler with ice and began pouring the vermouth. Skoal stepped behind the bar as if he were in a chemistry lab. He summoned everyone's attention as he instructed Heap in how to make the classic dry martini.

First, of course, he told him to fill a cocktail shaker with gin; then add a soupçon of dry vermouth and a few ice cubes. Stir the concoction gently; then strain the entire mixture into a big tumbler and add about six stuffed olives and a generous slice of the skin of the lemon. I decided then that Skoal invented the martini, because a long time passed before I ever again heard of anyone putting the skin of a lemon in a drink. Even then, Clara's theory probably made more sense: "Hah! That's so Paw and Ma'll think he's drinking lemonade."

Still, Skoal got his occasional comeuppance. In one of the bars, he sat next to an animated customer who was entertaining his companion with jokes about the English and their manners. Skoal, not to be left out, interceded by asking, "And are you English?"

The man, face reddening, snapped back in a strong brogue, "Do I drink beer from a straw?"

Oh, Skoal had him now.

"And you being what?" the man asked.

"Well, American, but my family's from Norway," Skoal said, rather too proudly. "And you're Irish. Why is it that Ireland is known to be the drunkenest country in the world?"

The man came head to head with Skoal. "Because, laddie, Ireland is full of shipwrecked Norwegians."

A New World's Record

For Uncle Skoal, fishing held far more fascination when it involved some additional challenge, especially if it implied danger. Skoal was described as "ready for anything." In short, he was tough—wooden leg notwithstanding. The pun, however, stands. Skoal made it well-known that he had boxed and wrestled in school. I kept thinking that if he had acquired the wooden leg early enough, he might have been a hell of a placekicker.

As I got older, "hell" started taking over for "heck," "damn" for "darn," and "bullshit" for "baloney." And Ella finally sprang the "F word" on me at school.

Skoal complained that freshwater fishing was for sissies. "These three-, four-pound fish. Phooey! I want a swordfish. I want to catch a seventy-pound marlin. Now that's a sport!"

All the same, he'd go all out to make our tame fishing as much of an adventure as possible. Leigh didn't much enjoy fishing with Skoal, who'd reject his expertise on time and location to pursue a route of his own, which is exactly what he was plotting on one memorable trip.

He'd usually drag me along—to my mother's horror—to

handle chores like baiting a hook, netting a fish, and opening a beer. While I enjoyed some of these outings, I really preferred going to the bars with Skoal over going fishing with him. I only wished Leigh or Torsti was with us to direct this particular trip.

Skoal figured that Torsti had been a bachelor long enough, so he'd take charge of his romantic life, even if Torsti did have a few years on him. Skoal said Tortsi's love life could charitably be called "nonexistent"; he was always devising some plan to get Torsti into the mix, as he put it. But Skoal complained, "Those sisters of his are always fixing him up with another 'ni-ice Svedish herring choker from da Lut'urn church.'"

"Well," I said, leaning on my wisdom, "Torsti's Finnish, and he probably—"

"Nah, Snowball, all those sardine sliders are alike. I finally did get Torsti out on a date. You know about that?"

"Oh-oh, not the Ferris wheel?"

"Who told you?"

"I investigated."

"Yah. I don't know. You don't know anything."

"No, just the part where you stand up on the Ferris wheel."

"The place was so crowded, four of us had to climb into one chair. The girls were hockey players from Eveleth. They can do anything. Near the top, I get thirsty. We had some cool ones in our pockets. I decapped 'em and chugalugged.

"Oh, man, Snowball, then I really had to go—g-o. Got to the very tip-top, and I stood up, and—I'll tell you—I thought my stream would be so strong it would go over the tops of everyone below us. Well, not quite. Torsti starts moaning that we'll all be arrested. But how the hell way down there they gonna know who did it? But Torsti was right. I was wearing my old maroon and gold sweatshirt. I whipped it off and dropped it through the back of the chair. Where it landed I do not know.

"You know something, Snowball, those chairs ain't all that safe. Very unsteady. I'm going to complain about that."

"Skoal!" I said as loud as I could. "Where the hell we going? You're getting way out of the fishing waters."

Skoal snapped back, "Don't you want to hear the rest of my story?" Then he smiled deviously, "And I've got half a mind to tell your mummy you said 'hell'.

"So, okay, so the Ferris wheel landed—smack, rattle—and I didn't waste a thin second before I shouted at the guy who unbuckled us, 'Those chairs are not too secure, buddy boy. You gonna have a bitch of a lawsuit on your hands if they get any wobblier! I know what I'm talking about. I'm a carpenter.'

"'Yah! Yah!'" Some jerk pointed at me, "'There he is. There he is. He's the one in the maroon sweater.'

"I turn around, and this dame throws the sweater at me. 'He did it! He dropped this filthy thing on me.'"

Skoal said to her in a really humble voice, "I not from Minneesoota. From Helsinko. Torsti, tell nice people in good English. Teach in school English in Finnlan'."

Skoal slapped his porkpie fishing hat at me. "Now Torsti starts laughing so hard I thought 'Oh, my, God, they're gonna put us all in jail.'

"You won't believe this, Snowball. Torsti points to the guy

who's with this dame and says, '*He* was wearing that maroon and gold Minnesota sweater when we boarded this rat trap.' Ahhhh, Torsti really got in the mood.

"I looked at the guy, sympathetic, and said, 'Probably only hold you overnight. Just say you can't hold it. You got 'inconsequence' or something like that. My ma got that problem, too. Very common.'

"Then we start walking away. The woman shrieked, 'Arrest him!'

"I turned back, and politely said to the guy, 'You'll be glad you got that sweater. Overnight, those jails really get cold.'"

Skoal was intrigued with a narrow channel into our lake just behind Turnaround Island where we picnicked. The channels between the lower and upper lakes were much larger. Leigh always warned him off. "Turnaround" was called that because turning around was just about impossible once committed to entering the channel. We took canoes through this shallow outlet without having to portage for hours. We camped on these farther shores, reaching uncharted lakes that had no houses, cabins, or saunas on or near them. Often, we wouldn't even see other boats. But we were always careful to return to our own lake before dusk.

Skoal and I were trolling for fish when we came upon this channel, which was totally unknown to him. He turned instantly into it, ignoring my warning that unless you were in a canoe, you needed to go a great distance before you could turn around. And trying to back up was more threatening than going ahead.

Uncle Skoal was fond of saying things like, "So what're you afraid of?" which I hated hearing.

Now I knew we wouldn't be getting back to the house until *after dark,* and my mother would start shuffling and rumbling about me being lost at sea. She had a right, in a way. She grew up on Lake Superior, which is like a sea, and men she knew disappeared in storms and accidents. The memory of a Great Lakes passenger freighter that was never found forever haunted her.

"Just like Nels," she'd say, though Great-Aunt Ingaborg never really explained how Nels had "disappeared forever." That case was too remote even for Snooplock.

We entered a muddy-watered pond so thick with weeds, cattails, lily pads, and shore grass that at times we had to shut down the motor, pull it up out of the water, and use oars to push our way through. We were in a trench so narrow that my oar sank into the mud flats so fast and so deep that we splashed about, bobbing up and down, and the top of my head was wet by the time I was able to pull the oar up again.

That's when Skoal saw it, the gigantic shadow of a fish in the shallow flats. Sometimes a school of mud minnows can fool you and create a formation that looks like a single huge fish. But when Skoal poked his oar at the mound, it thumped solid, then moved just enough for us to realize it was a living thing—an enormous living thing.

Skoal scrambled through the fishing tackle box for the largest hook he could find. It looked like he'd taken it right off the captain's arm in "Peter Pan." He pulled up our catch of sunfish that were hanging over the side of the boat. He baited the hook with a small, perfectly eatable sunfish in its own right, and dangled it in front of the monster just below us with its tail slithering slightly under the boat.

As our eyes adjusted to the dark water, the creature seemed to have grown still larger. So did my eyes. I remember shouting, "He must weigh more than I do!"

Skoal told me to shut up. "You'll scare him away."

I couldn't imagine a fish this large in a freshwater lake, and we figured we were about two-thousand miles from an ocean. The closest I'd gotten to an ocean was Omaha.

Skoal was getting angry over the monster's indifference to the feast he was pushing in its snout. He reached his hand down deep into the water.

"I can feel its back. It's more than two feet wide."

With a back that big, its mouth, open, could be the size of a basketball. I thought about Uncle Skoal having only one leg, and now he could lose a hand.

Skoal held me by the back of my pants as I hung over the side to look down into the fish's face. The fish was the same color as the mud, with its gills fanning unenthusiastically, reminding me of Aunt Ingaborg in her rocking chair. Its mouth puckered like a fat person out of breath, and I could imagine it muttering at the measly sunfish bait perched in front of it.

What seemed like millions of minnows swarmed around the great fish as if it was some neutral island they were exploring. The fact was, this fish probably had so much to eat in his private pond that it wouldn't bite on our bait even if

Skoal pried open its mouth and stuffed the sunfish down it.

By now Skoal was stomping his feet with frustration, using a lot of swear words that were new to me, although I still retained exclusive rights to "criminy."

Skoal announced, "We're gonna net it!" He grabbed our largest net, which at best could accommodate a thirty-pound northern pike, and that would be stretching it, literally.

Again, Skoal held me over the side to get a better idea of how we could pull in the monster without its cooperation. I couldn't get the net around its head because it was wallowing deep in the mud at the very bottom.

Skoal started to remove his pants, exposing his wooden leg. He was wearing a bathing suit. He told me to do the same. At the lake, I always wore a bathing suit under my pants, even when I went to Sunday school. In Minnesota, you never know when you might go swimming.

Skoal said we'd lift the fish into the boat, with or without its help. We went over the side. His wooden leg seemed to sink faster than the other one as he reached up to take an oar. He ordered me to prepare to grab the tail end of the fish.

Skoal raised the oar over his head. I shouted as he brought it smashing down on top of the head of the great fish, again and again. Skoal tried to grip the monster by its prickly gills, while I pulled up on the tail. We were slipping on the muddy bottom of the lake, and the great fish rolled us over more than once. I tried grasping it again and expected the giant to come alive at any second and turn on us like a smorgasbord.

Finally, slipping it into the boat, the fish almost filled it. We kept it as centered as possible, balanced so the boat wouldn't turn over. I sat straddled on the rails and pulled my feet up in case "Moby" attacked.

The fish sank our boat deeper in the mud, which required both of us to push our way out of it with the oars. When we reached water deep enough to put the motor down, I held my oar like a lance in case the monster suddenly came to life and had a perfectly understandable hankering for revenge.

At the moment, I wouldn't have minded at all seeing it take a small nip out of the only real leg Uncle Skoal had left.

Skoal had "caught" a record carp. His photograph with the great fish, which weighed almost sixty pounds (the all-time record then was about seventy-five), appeared in newspapers all over Minnesota, including the *Minneapolis Tribune*, where his bowling team would see it, and as far as the *Milwaukee Journal* in Wisconsin. Of course, the papers in the small lake towns printed the picture, too.

Skoal somehow was able to reel in copies of all of them, or so it seemed. Carol May and I spread them out on the living room floor, and we were all—yes, even Clara—down on our hands and knees reading about the battle of the carp and the wooden leg.

Skoal decided, that, out of jealousy, I was "the big mouth bass" who told all the papers about his wooden leg. The papers didn't know I was in on the caper. Another secret locked away forever in that bulging Norwegian closet.

Skoal couldn't have agreed more readily when Otto and Leigh warned him not to mention my involvement. Leigh knew instantly that the carp hadn't been caught with angling skills. By now, the game warden, a pal of Leigh's, knew as well, but all the publicity made it impossible for the authorities to act. Netting or trapping a carp was against the law, of course; the law required that it had to have been caught by bait and hook. All the same, the warden and the sheriff made sure that Leigh knew they knew so that Leigh could pass it on to Skoal.

Skoal handled his newfound notoriety with aplomb to spare. I, of course, was totally ignored in any description of his heroic feat. He drove to Grand Rapids to be interviewed, because we didn't have a telephone at the lake, and the people who tried to find us at the lake all got lost. "Everyone takes the wrong prong," Leigh said, just as happy that they did.

Lake Fishing magazine set up a telephone interview with Skoal through the Grand Rapids daily paper to find out what bait and equipment he'd used. *Ouch!* I was more impressed when Cedric Adams, who was more famous than anyone else in all of Minnesota, wrote a squib called "Nothing to Carp About." And on his WCCO radio show, he said, "Someone is always finding that old carp."

But good old Skoal didn't care. He enjoyed the suspicious questions, like how he happened to have a test line with him that was strong enough to pull in a fish that size. And how did the carp get so beaten up?

"Well, I was all alone, so it was quite a struggle. Took me three hours to pull it in. He got battered on the rocks, but I hung tight. Then getting him over the sides of my small boat was a challenge I won't soon forget."

Knowing Uncle Skoal, we all thought he might add that he'd lost his leg in the battle, too, just like Captain Ahab.

The Dog with the High-Heeled Feet and the Umbrella on Her Head

As a child, I always had dogs, and I memorialized them all by dedicating a poem to each. Never having thrown anything away, I still have copies of these epics.

They served me well in school, especially in high school, where our English teacher, Dorothy H. Mibrath, was not only a published poet but also an animal rights crusader. Writing poems was never a requirement, so I received a decided boost for going beyond the call of duty and even won first prize with a poem printed in the annual *Anthology of High School Poetry*.

My dogs were almost all mutts and strays, giveaways and pickups, who came into my childhood in this order: Shep, Mickey, Nebby, and Bunny. The dogs stayed at the lake most of the time, boarding with the Schumachers and occasionally with the Brodeens, but only with Alley Babba's permission. Torsti considered Shep as much his as mine, since we found him in the region. Sometimes I'd sneak a dog home to Minneapolis for short stays before returning to the lake.

Shep, I'd guess, was a kind of makeshift collie with a marvelous nose. A strong German shepherd influence from his parentage was pretty obvious. He was not a lost dog. I'd guess he was simply dumped out on a country road by someone. He had no collar and no tags. And we became inseparable.

Shep was much too big to sit on my lap, where he soulfully wanted to be seated. Instead, he'd rest his huge shepherd's head with his long collie face on my lap, and when we ate, he'd patiently tuck in under the table between my legs.

Sarah Schumacher, who understood animals and kids a whole lot better than she did grownups, thoughtfully analyzed Shep's psychiatric condition: "He has to be close to you at all times. If he could, he'd be close enough to hear your heart beat. To hear you breathe. If nothing else, then just to smell you. So he'll know he'll never be abandoned again. That is the greatest fear all animals have: being abandoned."

Mickey, a Heinz 57 if ever there was one, was short-haired and long-eared, and he was small and brown and scrappy. He was a harmless and happy dog. Like all animals, he claimed his turf. Given his size, his turf was strictly on the floor.

He especially loved it when I'd get down there with him.

I developed a canine voice for Mickey, and I'd have him say, "Hey, what are you doing down here on my floor? Are you looking to be licked—or do you want your ears washed?" Then I'd rub his white belly and stroke his brown back. I'd roll him over and give him a vigorous, wrestling massage. And he'd say, "More, more, more!"

Nebby, as white as Grandma's hair, might have had relatives in the dachshund clan. He was toylike and very loving. I named him "Nebby" after Nebuchadnezzar, whom I learned in Sunday school ran some really old country, like Babylon, long before President Roosevelt ran ours. I just liked his name.

Nebuchadnezzar, having the longest name of any of my dogs, merited the longest poem I wrote. The first stanza alone read:

> It was the last of October, quite an ordinary day.
> The time was at noon, and the weather just okay.
> Yet sure as we know that the sun goes down,
> And darkness closes in from all around,
> There was something unusual, something immense.
> You couldn't quite see it, just something you sense.
> For on this very eventful day, a new life was born,
> The life of a dog, who grew up to be—
> On the top of the list of my ancestral tree.

But we were all most in awe of Bunny, largely because she actually came with *papers* authenticating her as a purebred poodle. She was given to my grandfather, Pa, in exchange for his painting a NO TRESPASSING notice for some angry folks in Edina, a Minneapolis suburb where a lot of "swells" lived. Pa had his own sign shop, Show Cards & Signs, and wanted to become better known in this high-end community. Paying for goods or services with something of value other than money was not uncommon. I can remember my mother trading her mother's ornamental antique cut-glass dishes for a piano.

Pa scoffed at the petite puppy—well, she *was* French—and said her ears made her look more like a rabbit than a dog, which moved Aunt Dora to exclaim, "She's our own Easter bunny!" So in a burst of imagination I named her "Bunny."

But Grandma would have nothing to do with this peculiar *hund,* lest she pee or, worse, poop on Grandma's deep, wool Norwegian carpet artfully patterned in the homeland colors. And according to Dora's translation, Pa had taken to calling Bunny a "French hare" in Norwegian.

Dora, now a ranking star in the army—so much so that she was not allowed to reveal her next assignment—ordered a family council. We all obeyed instantly. The family council excluded in-laws like my mother. My father had a proxy vote that he refused to honor; it didn't matter because any way he voted would have irritated someone. I was eligible, but not Aunt Signe's husband, George, who *owned* a hardware store. Owners, of anything, were generally honored in the family. But, alas, Uncle George—who had what we called a "Nazi dog," a German shepherd called "Baron"—was not a blood relative, and Dora whispered to me that he hated "fussy toy dogs anyway, so good riddance." Baron, I was certain, would look upon Bunny as he would a sardine appetizer. Signe, Dora, Grandma, Pa, and I ordained that Bunny would be awarded exclusively to me.

Bunny was not even as big as the Brodeen sisters' cat, Alley Baba, and when she curled up, she was about the size of a basketball—a black, fur-covered basketball, to be sure.

Even though Bunny was as loving as any dog I'd ever owned, she had a lofty and unpredictable side to her. I attributed this special temperament to her all-poodle pedigree. I was sure she'd know I understood, since I was all Norwegian and temperamental, too. Also, I found out that poodles had been attendants to the court of the dippy old French Louis—and tended to be persnickety.

And Bunny was too genteel to be much of a country dog. Her pitch-black fur had the consistency of downy flakes, so when we returned from a stroll in the woods, she almost always required a bath to extract the ticks, burrs, and mud from her body, even inside her ears.

Her ears, in fact, only added to the confusion about her legendary breed. One ear went up while the other went down. They also tended to loop like wings instead of hanging evenly, like the ears of the poodles in all the pictures we collected in our desperation to find one with any resemblance to Bunny.

Still, after Bunny was groomed and given the traditional poodle cut, she'd strut down the street so proudly I called her "the dog with the high-heeled feet and the umbrella on her head."

As she grew, her resemblance to the breed verified on her certificate became increasingly suspect. Even the veterinarian asked us, "What kind of a dog is it, anyway?"

That question began to bug me like a bee in the outhouse. Finally, instead of explaining ("Yah, well, she's supposed to be a poodle . . . "), I improvised a new breed and declared emphatically that she was a "poobbit." Everyone seemed to be delighted to see such a rare breed and generally agreed that poobbits had some resemblance to rabbits.

Since Bunny possessed a certificate that demonstrated she was a member in good standing of the Society of American Poodles (SAP), Dora shot off a letter to them, demanding to know if we could expect some retribution if, indeed, Bunny was a fraud—"passing for poodle," so to speak. "If Bunny was misrepresented as a member of the Society of American Poodles, what course of action can we take?" Dora inquired.

The Society's response was even less cordial than Aunt Dora's indictment, demanding a detailed description of Bunny's ears, eyes, nose, feet, and tail, as well as her weight, height, and length of her legs. SAP also asked for photographs, both close-ups and long shots—full face, profile, front, back, sides, rear, overhead, and under.

Our investment in Bunny continued to go up as her stature went down. This time the Society of American Poodles responded by withdrawing Bunny's membership and instructing us in no uncertain terms to return the registration certificate that declared her a poodle.

In part the letter read: "This is to inform you that after having conducted a lengthy investigation concerning the litter out of which your dog is part, the facts developed failed to reveal that this litter was pure bred to the satisfaction of the Society of American Poodles. We have therefore canceled the registration of this litter and all of its individuals." Except for the organization's name, this was quite literally the unvarnished and unedited statement.

Dora voiced it, and we all agreed that this was a mean-spirited metaphor for making any judgment about any creature, animal or human, based on anything other than character. Sadly, we were all brought down by this development, and I could sense that Bunny's initial awesomeness was diminished in the eyes of her once-proud beholders.

Clara comforted me by saying, "Well, honey, she doesn't smell like a regular dog, so she must be sort of a show dog that wins medals." Always the cook, Clara added, "Bunny has a bit of a nutty aroma, like roasted pecans." My favorite nut, of course. Even Bunny's breath was sweet. Well, maybe not quite sweet, but unnoticeable. And she never farted.

Henceforward, Bunny would be identified exclusively as a purebred poobbit. Dora and I tucked her poodle certification among the rhubarb stalks where she always wet, just outside the lakeside door. After a good dousing, we let the certificate dry in the sun and then mailed it back to the Society of American Poodles.

Rhea's a Jew? What's a Jew?

The Schumachers seemed to have arrived from Germany "with only the shirts on their backs," as Clara exclaimed often enough. This observation seemed to contain a mystery for me, and nothing provoked old Snooplock's imagination more than that.

The family had spent some time in Canada before being able to come into the States. Minnesota adopted them under the auspices of a Scandinavian American rescue program that prevented immigrants from being turned away. Canada had been more accommodating than the United States.

Aunt Dora, who was forever exploring conundrums, observed that Mrs. Schumacher, Rhea, became visibly distressed when the subject of their leaving Germany came up. Mr. Schumacher, as I always addressed him, became sort of proud and aggressive.

Dora said, "Look how he holds her whenever you ask about life in Germany. He takes her by the shoulders and pulls her to him, like he's protecting her."

Out of my hearing—or so she thought—Dora concluded that Rhea was Jewish, and that the family had fled Germany fearing that she'd be arrested. Even before the war started in Europe, Dora explained, Jews were hated in Germany, and those who hadn't left were being sent to what she thought were called "work camps."

Rhea was quite shy, and Dora went out of her way to bring her into the center of any family gathering. This was a gesture Dora often made with people, which I thought even then was admirable. She and Rhea were about the same age and became good friends. She confided to Dora that when the family first settled in Minnesota and began meeting people, she was frightened all the time. "People keep saying 'Hi!' to me and raising their hands," Rhea said. "I thought they were saying 'Heil!'—and I wanted to hide."

We learned much later that Mr. Schumacher asked Dora not to tell anyone his wife was Jewish because she was afraid people would turn against her. She was terrified that someone would find out.

I didn't understand what being Jewish had to do with leaving your own country. Nor did anyone explain it to me satisfactorily. It seemed to embarrass them, as if it would hurt Mrs. Schumacher, whom we all liked very much.

As I tried to work these things out, I wondered if being a Jew was simply like being a Methodist or, even more exotic, a Catholic, which, as far as I knew, there were few of in Minnesota. Would that be enough to force you to leave your own country? Or worse, lock you up?

I could tell that Clara and Leigh weren't sure what being a Jew was either. Were they Protestants like us? I wondered. I knew Germans who belonged to our church.

When mother told Great-Aunt Ingaborg that Rhea was a Jew, she slapped her hand in a scolding gesture. "Ver you been living?" she said; then she confused matters more by saying that in Norway there were Jews who were just as Norwegian as we were. "Germans, Italians, everyone can be Jews."

Even Swedes? Although that sounded a bit farfetched to Pa, who was still angry with Sweden for allowing the German army access to invade Norway. He frequently amused himself singing:

> *Ten thousand Swedes*
> *ran through the weeds,*
> *in the battle of Copenhagen.*
> *Ten thousand Swedes*
> *ran through the weeds,*
> *chasing one Norvaygan.*

Clara and Leigh declared that the whole thing about Rhea having to leave her ancestral land where she was a citizen was simply outrageous. None of us could comprehend that you could hate people who had done you no harm and were totally unknown to you.

"It's just nuts!" Clara said, "And about the dumbest thing I've ever heard of."

Grandma's White Buffet

The lake house with its barn and sheds and outhouse, its wood-burning stove and pump water and kerosene lamps, was just too primitive for my Grandmother Anderson.

But on those rare occasions when she felt up to a weekend at the lake, she'd instantly commandeer the kitchen to prepare her ritual Sunday buffet, which she held in her south Minneapolis home for about fifty years. On holidays, the buffet was upgraded to a smorgasbord, which would be known today as a cholesterol blowout. Leigh, as a childhood friend of my father, remembered being invited many times. Aunt Dora's playmate, Harriette Lake, would occasionally be at Grandma's house in Minneapolis. A pretty, perky Danish girl, Harriette Lake lived across the street from nearby Lake Harriet. True. She was very talented—singing, dancing, acting, acrobatics. She went into show business, and Dora kept up with her. Harriette changed her name several times and finally settled on Ann Sothern when MGM made her a great star.

Grandma was a lovely-looking woman with a glorious bundle of white angel hair that she wore in a big bun, supported by mother-of-pearl pins and combs. She looked like the poster girl for a box of old-fashioned candies. Before going to bed, I sometimes caught a glimpse of her after she had released this cascade of hair, which flowed like the snow-falls of the fjords. An awesome sight.

She was born in Oslo, Norway, but her English was much clearer than Pa's, my grandfather, even though he was a commercial artist with a great deal of contact with the public. When Grandma would summon him to the buffet table, he'd say, "Yimmy cur-ickets, yew always start yust ven *Amos an' Andy* cum on da box."

Certainly the most memorable thing about those buffets was the blizzard of white on white—from the linen table-cloth to the huge napkins, the porcelain pots, the serving dishes, and the big snowballs of flowers. Almost without exception, the food itself was also white. A bounty of blanc victuals: a blaze-bleached fish; the vegetables, a puree of peroxide; and the desserts, a frosty forest.

A fairly routine buffet would feature at least twenty items. But what can you do? Some favorite is always missing. You just can't find good smoked reindeer tongue here like you can in Vimanshisttagard.

My grandmother felt that no one knew how to cook Norwegian food anymore—not Scandinavian food, mind you. *Norwegian!* She didn't care for Clara's cooking, which we all loved. "Mishmash," she called it. Clara, whose parents were born in Sweden (shush!), shocked my grandmother with all her brown food and worse—green, yellow, blue, and red vegetables, fruits, and desserts. And all those foreign spices and herbs from places like India and Africa.

Grandma guardedly commented on my mother's cooking to avoid creating still another bump in her son's marriage. She didn't even like the one dish my mother was admired for—gravy. Mother's gravy was dark, and grandma only tolerated white gravy.

In fact, I think my grandmother invented white gravy, because the only place I'd ever seen it was at her buffets, where it overwhelmed snowbanks of mashed potatoes. In fact, mashed potatoes were the secret ingredient for any number of dishes—bread, for example. And my favorite—thick, white sausages *(potatis korv)* that burst when pierced with a fork. Someone said they were like eating helium in a balloon.

Lutefisk was to Grandma's buffets what President Hoover was to America dour, sour, bland. It inspired a lot more "uff das" than "yummies." Grandma ventilated a huge bag of codfish with a long-handled fork, then unloaded it into a kettle of boiling water. She made periodic assaults on the fish with the fork to test its doneness. Did I say *done?* The smell of the glossy white chunks announced their entrance on the smorgasbord stage.

According to John Louis Anderson's (no relative) delightful book, *Scandinavian Humor and Other Myths,* lutefisk, by definition, "is codfish dried on racks in the icy Nordic air, and then soaked in lye, a major constituent of Drano and old-fashioned, homemade soap."

The secret agents of all this whitening were cream, powder,

milk, gravy—and peeling, boiling, bleaching, and blanching. Creamed herring and creamed fish balls (*fiskeboller*) remain the pale centerpieces for the appetizers, along with potato dumplings (*potet kaker*) and potato bread (*potet brød*). Swedish meatballs (*kjøttboller*) coated in white gravy were always dependable participants at these events.

Lefse, a thin flatbread usually cooked on a griddle, was always a strong supporting player. It was maneuvered into shape with a *lefse* stick, a sort of wood paddle.

The eccentric exception to this pallid pastiche was a block of what I knew as *gammel ost,* meaning "old cheese." And it really meant it. Apparently, gammel ost was white when first produced and smelled a lot like old limburger.

Gammel ost eventually turned yellow, and the smell of it became all the more pungent. No one ever described it as having an "aroma." It seemed to move and shape itself as it squirmed into its final greenish-brown stage. If you put a hunk of it on your buffet plate, its odor and flavor would permeate its neighbors—even taking over the flavor of lutefisk!

I always waited for Pa to say, "Dat's gewd gammel ost." Then I'd chime in, "Yah, Grandma, dat's gewd gammel ost."

This elicited so much snickering from my brother and my cousins that the adults shushed everyone up with their frosty looks. On occasions like these, which were all too frequent for my grandmother, she'd turn slit-blue eyes at me and declare in favor of my brother, "Bobby is the bestest boy." And he really was. He got out of almost everything by never getting involved in the sort of hapless risks I'd take.

For dessert, Grandma brought out mountains of snow-capped puddings: tapioca, bread, custard, rice, cream, marshmallow, and cabbage—yes, a pudding. Crispy cookies in a fragile shade of off-white in a variety of shapes: round, square, oval, triangular, star, heart, and diamond. But not to worry. They'd be sprinkled with clouds of powdered sugar, coming down like the first brush of an early blizzard.

At Christmas, Grandma made specialties with names that I loved to say because I thought they were so funny. *Fattigmann,* pronounced "futtimon," which means "poor men." They were a sort of deep-fried cookie, paper-thin and diamond-shaped. And *julekake* (Christmas bread), which to my ear was "yewla kawka."

My father's tastebuds were essentially done in by the time he got to dessert. After one hearty buffet, he raided the icebox later and ate a big dish of white margarine, which he topped with sugar and cream. He thought it was leftover pudding.

Back when my brother and I were emerging from toddlerhood, my grandmother unfailingly delivered unto us *white* chocolate candy bars. I was already a dark chocolate *junkie* before the word was coined. Even then I knew I wasn't exactly Grandma's "cat's meow."

That must have been one of the occasions when I resolved to make a record of any memorable event in my life. On a large lined tablet, in bold Palmer letters, I printed, BE MAD AT GRANDMA. I referred to this reminder for at least three more encounters with an unpitying grandmother who no doubt gave the world white fruitcake.

It's a Keeper!

As I was getting old enough to make more ambitious outings, nothing excited me more than taking a canoe trip out of Ely, Minnesota, with Leigh or one of my buddies, Jim Ledwein, who was probably the most gifted angler of us all. We'd go as far as the Canadian border and sometimes into Ontario to fish the fabulous Lake Nipigon.

Once the canoe was in waters like these, portaging from one lake to another was seldom necessary. In this vast north country with its often uncounted and sometimes uncharted waters, stretches of land between lakes seemed to be fewer than stretches of lake between land.

The lakes here were like aquatic trails, and it remained magical to me that deep in these forested acres, often inaccessible by road, a shallow outlet emerged giving birth to still another waterway. Early morning is so beautiful. Dew still clings to the leaves and a fragile curtain of mist won't quite let the sun come through. The lake itself is still shivering, but a silver path would be so distinct that I felt as if I could step out on it and walk across the water.

On one of these ventures, Leigh and I came upon a lake that was unknown to us, at least unnamed on the map. We secured at a dock that looked as if it could use my old crutches to hold it up. Leigh was unpacking the canoe. The tableau caught the shifting patterns of blue water and green shore. Leigh's face seemed to unwrinkle at times like these, and his expression glazed over as if he were dreaming.

Did I learn something about serenity then? If I did, it had not yet reached my conscious mind. Many years later, I traveled on assignment with the poet and Lincoln biographer, Carl Sandburg, and he talked about "creative solitude." I knew exactly what he meant. Visions of this sort have stayed with me all my life, especially when I'm drifting off to sleep and searching for a peaceful thought.

Leigh and I were soon catching much larger fish than we were used to getting in our lake, where I'd want to hang on to any fish I caught, however small. But that depended on a ruling on Leigh's part, both a moral and a legal judgment that he'd make with great solemnity: "It's a keeper."

Those three words thrilled me. Leigh grinned widely. I'd literally cheer and do everything but dance on the water. So much for somber and silent Scandinavian fishermen.

On this trip I hooked one of the most memorable fish I've ever caught (not too fierce a competition)—a ten-pound walleye, which is about as big as this most exquisite freshwater delicacy gets. In fact, ten- to fifteen-pound walleyes are practically trophy fish.

And he was a beaut, like the perfect specimen illustrated in an L.L.Bean catalog. A walleye this size has a very broad back, and we had to net it to get it in the boat. I used both hands to hold the fish as Leigh extracted the hook.

I cradled the huge fish in my arms as if I were holding my dog. "He must weigh more than Bunny," I said. "He's heavier." He was, by three pounds.

The next morning, of course, we planned to pack up and head for the nearest fishing lodge, where we'd get our catches packed in dry ice. Lodges often took photographs of an impressive string of fish like ours. My plan was to present this prize walleye to the Schumachers. "It'll feed the whole family," I told Leigh.

"Well, there are fourteen of 'em," he said. "Maybe we'll throw in a couple of mine."

Leigh, of course, had already caught quite a few more than a couple. He outfished me by about five keepers to one. When I had a good bite, he'd secure his fishing rod to stand by if I needed any help reeling it in. He'd never bully me with instructions. He was happier for me than if he had the fish on his own line. He taught me his methods without raising his voice, just as he later taught me how to drive a car.

The variety, range, and size of the fish we were catching were awesome. Here were lakes where northerns ran to thirty-five pounds and lake trout to as much as thirty-seven.

About the only dwelling of any kind on the lake was a fishing shack with a dock, which we figured belonged to a big lodge on one of the larger lakes in the region. We decided to tie up my glorious walleye, still very much alive, at the end of the dock in the deepest water where it would have ample room to remain fresh.

This resolved, we set up our tent near the shore, and Leigh, meticulous as always, dug a hole and reinforced it to create a safe fire. We had plenty of loose wood but no scraps or paper to get the fire going easily.

"Just gather some of that birch bark laying around," he told me.

It was still wet from a morning drizzle, but birch bark can be soaked and still catch fire.

Leigh had taught me how to clean fish, a task I avoided until he made it look easy. He called it "steaking a fish," and he performed the operation so skillfully that you didn't risk getting your throat pierced later by a small bone. He even severed the cheekbones from walleyes. They were Clara's favorite part of the fish, plump and tender.

After eating, we rigged our food supply to a tree branch out of reach of bears. I took one more look at my walleye and wondered if I should have it stuffed and hung over the fireplace at the lake. Skoal would find that hilarious. But I'd much rather make a show of it by personally presenting it to Sarah Schumacher.

At the first light of morning, I ran to the dock to marvel once again at my incredible catch. The fish seemed infinitely lighter as I carefully brought up the line. Then I came face to face with what was left of my ten-pound prize. He had been eaten alive, no doubt by turtles. I was much too old to cry. Leigh put his arm around my back and said, "Don't worry. That'd make a grown man cry." And we didn't even have a photograph.

Leigh tried to console me by saying losing the walleye was all his fault. "I was taking too many chances with the laws of nature," he said. "I should have known better."

I buried what was left of my walleye. I didn't want the turtles to come back. I wasn't sure I ever wanted to fish again.

We were heading for still another outlet to still another lake. That was when we saw our first moose, lazily bathing and drinking the water. We had to stop. There wasn't room for all of us, and even perched in the canoe with all our equipment, we felt about half the size of this magnificent beast.

Leigh thought the moose was at least six feet tall. A moose that big weighs more than a thousand pounds. It has broad, flat antlers that could hang a lot of coats and a short neck with an overhanging muzzle. Ugly, no! He was awesome. We could have watched him all day. But he slipped into the channel, swimming ahead of us. Moose are so strong and formidable that nothing challenges them, except the increasing proximity of the automobile.

The moose took my mind off my walleye, but as soon as it was out of sight, I lamented, "I'll never get another one like that." And I never did.

But Leigh was determined to cheer me up. That was when he'd call me Curt, instead of kid. I liked that. *Leigh and Curt.* He recognized that I'd aged on that trip, even in the last few hours.

"You know, Curt"—he repeated my name comfortably, like old friends—"some of those songs we sang with the barbershop quartet—well, there were a few of them we didn't sing in front of the ladies."

That got my attention. Hey, I really was getting older.

These were songs, he explained, that were "a little off-color." Leigh's quartet sang them at all-male gatherings.

I asked him if they were sort of naughty, like "Three Little Maids from 'Par-ee.'"

"Something like that," he allowed.

In Leigh's hushed tenor, lilting and rhythmical, he taught me a few. To this day, my favorite remains "The Bearded Lady." Then, as we coasted gently on the currents of the channel, Leigh and I serenaded the scented woods and unseen wildlife:

> *Oh, I love the bearded lady*
> *'Cause her whiskers tickle so.*
> *Her whiskers make me prickle*
> *From my head down to my toe.*
> *Oh, that kiss with the moustache in it—*
> *It's no wonder I get passion-na-a-ate—*
> *I love the bearded lady*
> *'Cause her whiskers tickle so-o-o-o-o.*

Now that's a keeper!

Danger: Dead Lake

More often than not on these journeys, Leigh and I were the entire crew. With no family nearby, occasionally our conversation turned more intimate.

We were about thirty years apart in age but solidly committed to one another. Clara and Leigh could be having coffee in the kitchen and if I walked in, she'd turn to Leigh and with great warmth say, "Well, here comes your best buddy."

And I was. I really was—and so proud of it.

Even back in the city, we usually lived in close proximity to the Johnsons, although we moved so often I'd have to trek off to still another unfamiliar school and start all over to make new friends. I became despondent.

Finally, when my dad moved us from Columbia Heights to southeast Minneapolis, I rebelled. I wanted to be with my class, where I was active and popular. Going to school for me was not unlike the release I felt when we went to the lake. So by high school I frequently stayed overnight with Leigh and Clara.

It troubled Leigh that I didn't have a better relationship with my father. He was always trying to put something together to improve the situation. At one point, he told my father that he wished he had a son like me, a nice sentiment, a great compliment to my father and me.

"But you know what your dad said?" Leigh smiled, rather sadly. "He said, 'You practically have.' Your mother feels I take up too much of your time, too." She certainly felt I spent more time with Leigh than I did with my own family.

"Otto said he just couldn't understand it. He said you and your mother used to be such great pals."

"But my dad's got Bob," I blurted out, and immediately hated the way it sounded. I thought it was reassuring to my father that he and my brother saw eye to eye, both men's men, so to speak. Great sportsmen. Strong, silent, even shy.

Leigh encouraged my father to express himself more to me. "You know, youngster," he said, "most Norsks aren't very outgoing. Your dad has a really tough time talking about *feelings*. But I can tell you, he loves you, and he's darn proud of you. He says you're a lot smarter, reading books the way you do, even when you were just a kid. And fiddling away on that typewriter.

"You know, don't you, what your dad went through in the war? He had the stuffing knocked out of him. The infantry. Front lines. Gas. You saw that hole in the German helmet he keeps in that war trunk with his old uniform. Your dad shot that hole. When there was a head in it!"

"He never told me that," I said. "I used to play with it."

"Otto had all the stuff to be a major league player. He thought he was on his way. But they didn't pick him up from the farm team to pitch in the majors."

"You, too," I said. "You were his catcher."

Leigh leaned closer to me. "Your dad *cared* a lot more than I did. Like so many boys after these filthy wars. Older. Wiser. And maybe not as full of dreams as they were at seventeen."

Leigh explained that the Depression led to a lot of heavy drinking. "The bad times," he called them, "coming right off prohibition and after the war. The darnedest combination of ugly events I can think of. I'd probably be a drinker, too, if it weren't for Clara."

"About the only thing my dad ever tells me, 'Don't do what I do, just do what I say.'"

"Maybe not such bad advice."

"I never know what he means."

"Now you do."

I finally realized that Leigh had sort of taken me to the woodshed, in his own sweet time.

We were anchored near our beaver dam—"our," since we supervised the project. Meticulously constructed, beavers are efficient engineers with a distinct foreman and crew. Each task has a reason for being done. Here they were easing the currents that entered the outlet to their impeccable lair.

Leigh put up a chickadee feeder nearby as a sort of juke-box for the beavers. "Chick-a dee-dee-dee!" Once these small tame birds see a feeder, they know this is a friendly port and will likely eat out of your hand.

I'd become as comfortable as a Quaker with our long stretches of silence on the lake. Most people find that disconcerting and reach awkwardly for something to say. On a boat, your own silence also comes with the lovely silence of your surroundings. And it often enlarges your world with an invitation to reach for something larger to say.

This was often the case with us. Leigh broke into my thoughts, saying, "You know, Curt, sometimes I don't think you remember everything your dad has done for you."

I must have looked startled. He read my mind. Speaking so personally about my father led me to thinking of an event I often blocked. Just thinking of it made my skin crawl. Now I wanted to say it before Leigh did. "My dad saved me from drowning."

"Something like that's kind of hard to forget."

"My dad never mentions it," I said. "And my mother doesn't know it ever happened."

"Maybe we just like to think that some things never really happened."

But it did. It had been another one of those days on our lake when even the mosquitoes weren't biting. "I can't even get me a sunfish to throw back," Leigh had said.

He was studying his treasured little ring-bound fishing notebook, where he kept track of significant catches, favorite spots, bait shops, and lakes to try.

My father hated trying other lakes. Moving the boat and equipment was a major undertaking, and then having to search for some lake Leigh recorded in his book months ago, possibly years. But everyone who knew Leigh said his notes were as good as Indian tracking.

By late morning, Leigh, Dad, and I ventured onto a desolate lake unknown to us—no boats on the lake, not even what seemed like remnants of cabins. As far as we knew, it didn't have a name.

"Maybe you're the only one who's ever found it," I said. "Call it Lake Leigh."

"Not gonna name *this one* after me." Leigh didn't like the looks of the lake. The surface was dark and thick. "It's a messy, dirty lake. Full of junk."

When I got out to push the boat into deeper water, my tennis shoes instantly filled with guck. And then we were only able to go a few feet before we were stuck again.

"Let's not go out any more," Leigh said.

Dad swept his hand through the water and came up with muddy sand and dead weeds. Broken tree branches and loose bark further camouflaged the depth of the lake.

Leigh cupped his hand in the water, smelled it, and shook his head. "We've got a dead lake here. Should be posted."

He quickly reviewed his notes and crude landmarks he'd drawn. "Paw and I caught a few fish here. Remember what it was called. Rat Lake."

"*Rat?*" I said.

"I don't even think the rats have survived."

We didn't try to lower the motor into the water for fear of entangling the blades. "Otto," Leigh called out, "get up here with me and take the other oar."

Now two strong men were at the helm, leaning into those oars and pulling back, trying to turn around to head for the shore where we had arrived. But the lake itself seemed to control our direction.

More than once, Leigh told me, "When you're stuck, kid, you gotta get out and push."

So I decided to save the day. I must have known it was a really dumb decision, because I didn't ask for anyone's advice or permission. The simple fact is you don't get out unless you know how deep the water is.

I pulled the straps off my skinny shoulders and dropped my overalls. As I went off the back of the boat in my bathing suit, I heard Leigh shout too late, "No, no, Curt, not yet."

I intended to push the boat while the crew rowed, which almost always worked. My bare feet hit sand but did not stop there. I continued going down through a slide of grimy underwater. I'd never heard of quicksand in Minnesota, but it was either that or something damn similar.

I struggled with my arms and legs to reverse directions. By then I had swallowed so much sand and water I started gagging. I tried to open my eyes, but I was a prisoner in a whirling black hole. And the muck was so thick I couldn't see or hear anything.

Scrambling in any direction, I suddenly felt my hand breaking the surface of the water. My head hit the boat and back I sank. By then, I must have been under the boat.

I was swatted by something like a tree limb that turned out to be a bamboo fishing pole. I caught it and was pulled around to the side of the boat. With viselike strength, four arms grasped at my slippery skin. Then Leigh and my father struggled to reach the straps of my overalls that simply weren't there. Finally, a hand that felt like a giant crane gripped and pulled at the long entanglement of my white hair and, with the other hand, grabbed me by the chin.

I lost any awareness of what was happening. I was awake but where was I? The only sensation I felt was of being under fierce control of whatever force clutched me—and that I would not be lost. My father yanked me out of the water like the tassels of a sea bag.

I was crawling, not with rats, but with leeches, in my hair and on my back and legs. Leigh tried pulling the bloodsuckers off, then applied salt; some folks try burning them off with cigarettes. None of these methods are advised. Salt can get into the wound where the leeches draw blood. When my eyes cleared enough to see, Leigh was treating the bloody sores.

Then I felt the comforting bruising strength of my father's hands forcing me to cough up water and vomit sand. Leigh wrapped me in a towel. My father stared at me with an expression of such desperation that I wanted to cry. He covered me with his embrace and tried to speak, but couldn't.

The Best and the Brightest

I continued to spend my summers at the lake, even into high school, with the war raging at its peak. When the German army invaded Norway, the tension and concern increased. My parents both had relatives in Norway; my paternal grandmother had a brother with whom she had been very close. With the Nazi occupation of Oslo in 1940, Great-Uncle Olaf's department store was confiscated by the invaders and put in charge of some Norwegian "quisling," so named for a traitor. Olaf soon became active in the Norwegian underground. Grandmother's brother was destined for a concentration camp as an enemy of the Third Reich.

Then one Sunday we were urgently summoned to my grandmother's house in south Minneapolis. Her phone call had my parents whispering. I just assumed it was the usual Sunday buffet, when I always tried to slip away to see a matinee movie.

Great-Uncle Olaf had escaped from Norway in a British ship. From London, the Royal Air Force flew him to Canada, where he was given permission to visit the United States.

The British navy was extraordinary in making runs into the North Sea and rescuing thousands of Norwegians so they could fight again for the Allies.

I only saw Uncle Olaf on that one occasion, and I will never forget him. He had a cloud of whipped-cream white hair. An elegant man in a beautifully tailored suit, he had the commanding air of his sister, but with much greater warmth.

He chose not to embrace the safety of permanent residence in the United States and went on to serve with Norway's government-in-exile in London. The Norwegian merchant fleet distinguished itself fighting with the Allies. I was so proud to know Great-Uncle Olaf.

But the war itself didn't thrill me as it did so many other kids. I saw no adventure in it, just death and destruction. Hitler had given the world no other course, and countries sent off "the best and the brightest."

Bob couldn't wait to get into it. He enlisted the day he was eligible. I was glad I was still too young. Did that make me a coward, I wondered? Boys—yes, *boys*—not much older than I faced the numbing prospect of fighting in the brutal battlefields of Europe and the savage jungles of the Pacific. They were so young they screamed for their mothers when they were hit.

I was safe for a few more years until high-school graduation in 1946. By then the war was over, but the draft was still active. I enlisted in the navy amidst rumors of a war with Russia and that we were all going to be shipped to Alaska. Has the world gone mad? Or had that already happened? A reckless wing of the military and an extremist political-industrial base argued that the United States should fight Russia while our forces were still intact. Thank God we also had a great president, Harry S Truman, and a brilliant military commander, Dwight D. Eisenhower.

My brother, Robert Gerald Anderson, who was "Bob" to his family and "Huck" to his friends, even into his adult life, was made of the right stuff. In January 1945, in the Rhine Valley, Bob was wounded in the back and in his left leg. He spent six weeks in a hospital in Paris; then he was ordered to rejoin his unit back in Germany. The war in Europe ended in May and Bob was finally returned home from England, soon to be discharged, less than a month after his nineteenth birthday.

Another act of courage on his part is *still* buried in that deep, secret Scandinavian closet. The incident was never spoken of, and as far as I know, never revealed until this writing.

I was not yet eligible for a driver's license but was determined to make it to a date and make it impressive. This was not a date I even considered sharing with someone who could drive. Of course, I had no alternative but to take my father's car. Well, he simply wasn't there to ask for his permission.

On my way I approached a famously busy intersection, and the light was just turning red. But, of course, I thought I had plenty of time. Another driver relying on the same timing hit my dad's car smack on the passenger side.

Incredibly, Bob, who was home on leave, was standing just outside a famed hangout and witnessed the entire incident. He, of course, was stunned to see me in our father's car, and he could tell an accident was just about to happen. He motioned me frantically to stop before the certain collision.

He stealthfully made his way to the car and opened the door before I could. I was not injured, just shocked.

By the time I looked up, Bob was negotiating with the driver of the other car on the basis that he was equally at fault. *He? Bob?* Bob identified himself as the driver of Dad's car. The man who hit me appeared relieved. They exchanged insurance numbers. No need to call the police since it was a no-fault situation. Shook hands.

"Seems like a pretty nice guy," Bob said. "I think he's got some license problem himself." Then he pointed to a gas station on a corner a few yards away. "Buddy of mine runs that station. Bet he can pound out that little dent and match the paint."

Okay, so now you know. My father never did.

For many years I hoped Leigh would convert the lake place to a farm, as it had once been, and that I would be able to prevail upon my parents to let me live with Clara and Leigh, not just for the summer months, but permanently.

I wanted to work on the farm and go to school with the Schumachers. I would see my parents when Clara and Leigh drove down to their home in Minneapolis. This, of course, never happened. But I did leave home on my own, for about six months, when I was fifteen years old. By the time I returned to Minneapolis to finish school with my class, I finally realized, like Dorothy in *The Wizard of Oz*, that there is no place like home.

Before long I was spending less and less time at the lake. It wasn't so much that I outgrew my youthful passion for the place, but I started taking odd jobs and dating in earnest. I liked to usher in movie theaters where I could see good films—and bad ones—over and over again. I let all my friends in free through a side entrance. I was especially generous to a group of popular and pretty girls, who came to call themselves "the CCs," for the Century (the name of the theater) Clubbers. I also became more involved socially, dating and the like, and in a slew of school activities: editor of the Columbia Heights High School paper—the *Pocket Gopher*—and homecoming king. My hobbies, such as acting and writing for amateur theater, were taking more and more of my time. But I continued to write Sarah Schumacher with great devotion. We shared notes about our crushes and timid romances. In one letter she wrote in her gracefully bold handwriting, "I don't call anyone my *boy friend*, but if I had to call someone my boy friend, I would much rather call you my boy friend than another person who writes to me. He is too old. More than nineteen!!! You're still too young, but you're not as *much* younger than he is older. See what I mean."

We also exchanged pictures, and Sarah sent me a lock of her dark, silky hair at my request. No one quite measured up to Sarah, our princess. And I still entertained the illusion that she and I were somehow destined for one another. Unfortunately, I stubbornly continued to look about half Sarah's age, while she was getting taller faster and was filling out like a beauty queen.

Sarah and her brother Herb were the best and the brightest, too, certainly in their rural high-school class. Herb was just old enough to have a brief stint in the war, but not quite reaching his dream of being part of the forces that took back his home country.

When Sarah turned seventeen, Aunt Dora had the idea of writing a song for Sarah's birthday, and she enlisted Herb and me to help. The entire Schumacher clan, as well as her Pied Piper legions, accepted it as Sarah's anthem.

Dora got her inspiration from her idol. In the 1930s, Will Rogers was the most popular entertainer in America—and it's not too far-fetched to say that Dora worshiped him. He was the perfect poppa and big brother for her generation. Although her devotion seemed a bit exaggerated at times in order to lasso my grumpy grandpa's goat (to put it as Will Rogers might himself). Pa considered Will Rogers's *coda persona*—I never met a man I didn't like—about the sappiest thing he'd ever heard. "Vell, I've met plenty of 'em!" he enjoyed saying.

All this was just too rich in Scandinavian contrariness for us to ignore, so the three of us set out to celebrate Sarah's birthday with a song called, "I've Never Met a *Horse* I Didn't Like." Dora's hunch about her beloved Will Rogers was confirmed by our movie historians, Esther and Elsie Brodeen, who insisted that Will himself actually *liked* his horse more than any man he'd ever met. Elsie went absolutely razzmatazz over the number, and she dragged her brother, Torsti, to rehearsals because he had a banjo, admittedly more for plucking than playing.

But why, after salvaging just about everything I ever had a

whimper of affection for, *why* couldn't I find any trace of our snappy country lyrics for "I've Never Met a Horse I Didn't Like"? All that remains of this musical triumph are these few remnants that I am able to call up in my head, which may explain why no one saved it:

> *I've never met a horse I didn't like.*
> *I'd rather ride a horse*
> *Than take a hike.*
> *A pig'll only squeal*
> *'til he gets another meal.*
> *A cow'll chew her cud*
> *Even stuck in the mud.*
> *A chicken'll lay an egg,*
> *But only if you beg.*
> *And a goat'll keep on kickin'*
> *Even if he gets a lickin'.*

We had written lots more stanzas. Herb had a stinging little jingle about garter snakes. Sarah hated them because they scared the horses. And this rousing chorus followed each stanza:

> *But I've never—*
> *Not even* ever!
> *No, I've never met a horse I didn't like . . .*
> *No, sir!*
> *I've never met a horse I didn't like.*

(Note: In 1991 *The Will Rogers Follies*, a musical comedy, opened on Broadway and had a good run. The show's featured song, both the opening and closing number, was, of course, "Never Met a Man I Didn't Like." The song was very show-busy, uplifting, and much too pretentious. Will Rogers would have preferred our rambling little ditty.)

The Schumacher family's intense labors had finally rewarded them with a financially thriving farm, including a new house that Clara said was "so big that everyone must have a room of his own." Sarah now had a selection of horses to ride. I'd always ask about her horses, expecting to hear that she was losing her interest in riding as she grew older. Quite the opposite. In fact, she discussed opening a stable on her parents' property. She'd teach riding—and "equestrian care and training." In almost the same sentence, she also considered becoming a jockey. But she was growing too fast; she'd be much too big—and who ever heard of a female jockey? Well, there was always Elizabeth Taylor in *National Velvet*, a hit movie in 1944. Surely, Sarah would qualify for the rodeo circuit. She rode as hard and had as much control of a horse as any man. In fact, at times she seemed to ride as if she were free of the normal hazards that imperiled the rest of us.

When she wasn't riding or in school, she was still cheerfully guiding her younger siblings on how to grow up gracefully self-sufficient. And her followers were still as devoted to her as she was to them. Big sister Sarah ran a world of her own creation, in which she'd never be second-best.

A Wilderness of Flowers

Herb rarely crossed the lake to visit us, certainly not when I wasn't there. The precious few hours when he wasn't working in the fields or at school, he savored for his special pastimes. That's why Clara and Leigh were surprised to hear the unmistakable struggling sound of Herb's old outboard motor chugging across the lake.

Leigh said he focused his binoculars on Herb's face to be sure who it was. He had never seen such a look of anguish on this cheerfully optimistic young man. He attributed it to the fact that Herb had to keep tugging at the rope time and time again to keep the motor running.

Both Clara and Leigh hurried down the embankment to meet him. Herb tied up at the dock—"never taking his eyes off us," Clara said. "He seemed unable to say anything, and we weren't about to push him. But those huge dark eyes bespoke terrible pain."

Clara saw blood on his hand where he had been yanking on the rope. Not having full control, especially of some piece of machinery, was so unlike Herb. Clara rushed him up to the kitchen where she kept her medical kit on a pantry shelf in one of Leigh's big, white, high-button-shoe boxes.

Herb was silent while Clara washed his hand under the pump, then bandaged and taped it. His tanned, expressive face seemed suddenly sallow. Clara and Leigh were frozen with grim expectations.

While riding in the woods late the night before, Sarah had been struck in the head by a tree branch. Herb swallowed hard and said, "Sarah's dead."

Clara told me later, "I wouldn't have been more surprised if he told me it was the end of the world."

Now Herb, in his desperation to control his grief, seemed unable to stop talking. "She was taking a different trail. Not marked. Not really familiar. And she must have been—have been in a terrible hurry. Getting dark. It was getting real dark. It was already dark . . ."

Clara pulled the tall, husky boy into her arms. Leigh hugged his back with his other arm around his wife. Through deep breaths, Clara said, "I'll get my Bible. Tell your folks we're coming right over."

Don't we always know exactly where we were on occasions that are like freeze-frames in our lives? I was at school in an algebra class, which I hated. I didn't feel I was learning anything. The man who taught it didn't seem to be able to distinguish algebra from arithmetic. Also, his breath was so bad that when he leaned in my direction, all I could think of was Grandma's *gammel ost*.

The principal's secretary interrupted the class to announce within everyone's hearing that I had an "urgent telephone call." I had never been called out of a class before. I was thrilled; the kids looked at me as if she had said, "The White House is on the line." Then I had a flash of agonizing second thoughts. Why would anyone call me "urgently" at school unless it was bad news?

The secretary stared at me with narrowed, sorrowful eyes, as if she knew something. What was it? Then it struck me: "Oh, no. My brother's been killed in the war." She led me to a conference room where teachers' meetings were held. She said I could take the call in private.

It was Herb. "I don't know how to tell you this, but I have to. Sarah was killed—" He continued, but I had no idea what he was saying. "She was riding; you know how fast she'd get her horses to gallop. She knows those woods so well; and so do the horses. She even knew when to duck and when to slow down. But it was getting dark, and she must have gotten off one of her trails or tried a shorter way back to the farm." The boy who prided himself on never crying wanted me to know, "When Sarah died, I cried. Boy, did I cry."

I didn't cry then. I didn't even shout "*No!*" or "How could it happen?" I just yelled, "*Where is Sarah?*"

Herb kept talking for my sake. In his own despair, he wanted to reach out to me. He said that Sarah had stronger feelings for me than she ever let on. I felt the chair sinking into the floor. I even looked to see if it was the kind of chair that adjusted. Had I inadvertently touched some lever that lowered it? I was drained. I was falling.

All the harmony and beauty—and security—I had always associated with the lake was destroyed forever. We *did* get older—and now one of us was gone.

"God must have needed another angel," Herb said. He told me that Clara and Leigh were at the farm. Clara was preparing a meal for the family, so he'd better return home. He was telephoning from a neighbor's.

"And hey, Curt, we have a phone now. But I didn't want to make this call from home. Everyone's there."

Not much was said as the family gathered around the big kitchen table. Clara asked everyone to hold hands while she recited the Lord's Prayer.

I wish I'd been there. I know I would have handled myself better than on the telephone with Herb when I was shocked into silence. Afraid that if I'd said something it would all come out as choking gibberish.

Clara said offerings came from all the neighbors, teachers, church members, townspeople—many folks who had never met Sarah but knew about her from their children. Cakes arrived—and hot dishes, fresh walleye, home-baked bread, venison stew, an enormous ham, dozens of eggs, and fresh vegetables. So much, Clara said, that it looked like a farmers' market.

Herb took charge of distributing most of the food to dirt-poor families who lived along the river in tin shacks with tarpaper. That's when I knew there would always be poor people, whether or not the world in general was in a depression, in a war, or in riches.

After they finished eating, Rhea suggested that they go around the table, and anyone who wanted to think of some loving memory of Sarah should speak. Esther and Elsie were there. Instead of speaking, Elsie knew no one would love it

177

more than Sarah if she sang the song we had all made up and had even sent to Will Rogers: "I've Never Met a Horse I Didn't Like." It was difficult for anyone to laugh, but I know Sarah would just be roaring.

When Clara described the experience, I thought of one of the books Aunt Dora had given me that contained a eulogy that Robert G. Ingersoll wrote for his brother's funeral. I hoped he wouldn't mind my converting this passage for Sarah:

> *If everyone for whom*
> *she did some loving service*
> *were to bring a blossom to her grave,*
>   *she would sleep tonight*
> *beneath a wilderness of flowers.*

Sarah had once knitted me a bright-red wool winter cap with a white tassel. "Red for your blushing face, and white for your hair." The cap was big enough to pull down over my ears. It was only early fall and the weather hadn't turned cold, but I brought the cap to her funeral, holding it tightly, as if I were holding her hand.

Since the Schumachers had no established church, the Reverend Johnson, of course, presided. His sermon was unforgettable for all the wrong reasons. First, he drew a lengthy analogy between Sarah and a comic strip character called Invisible Scarlet O'Neil, who was popular at that time. It seemed Scarlet could just press her wrist and disappear, clothes and all. This way she avoided being victimized by the villains that pursued her day after day.

"Just like Scarlet O'Neil, Sarah pressed her wrist—and

disappeared. We don't see her, but we know she is still with us. Try to think of Sarah . . ."

Since the pastor still hadn't succeeded in alienating everyone, he finally came up with one last wisp of witlessness: "This beautiful and brave family can be grateful to have eleven of its twelve children still surviving. With illnesses and accidents, depression and war—and the odds being what they are, seldom does a family this large have so many left to succor and comfort."

Dora, who was close to Rhea and had adored Sarah, later said, "If ignorance was against the law, that preacher would be doing twenty years to life in Stillwater."

I longed for someone like Great-Aunt Ingaborg to talk to. What would she have said? "Don't cry for your loss; cry for the loss of a lovely life struck down in her beautiful youth."

I had realized for some time that I was more like Inga than anyone else, even Leigh. Those words I imagined Inga saying were exactly how I felt: Sarah did not get to experience life beyond a foreshortened youth. I still wince when I read of someone so young dying of any cause.

The hurt lingers over the years, fading and returning in sudden, jarring moments when I think of Sarah and stop whatever I'm doing. Even walking on a street, I will blurt out, "Oh, God, no, please!"

Still I will always see Sarah, astride her golden steed, looking imperiously somewhere beyond the woods, as if she knew something was ahead for her that the rest of us would not be sharing. And I find comfort knowing in my heart that Sarah will always be galloping through those blueberry summers.

EPILOGUE

Gifts I Keep Getting

At the opening of these pages, I wrote, "It seemed to me our blueberry summers would never end. No one would really age. I would remain eight, nine, ten, or twelve, at most. The blueberry patches, as onerous and glorious as life itself, would continue to stroll along our trails, climb our hills, and saunter down our valleys."

But we all have to let go of childhood. My wish would have been that those blueberry summers would simply drift away serenely and that those parts that were magic would remain vivid enough to me that I'd always be able to look back on them and smile.

I think that happened.

Clara and Leigh and my parents maintained the longest-running friendship I have ever known, and they remained as different as sunlight is from shadow. While Clara and my mother continued to be competitive, even for my affection, it comforted me that these women—so far apart in character and spirit—together with my father and Leigh, clearly brought a great deal of happiness to one another.

My parents needed the amiable and optimistic lifestyle that Clara and Leigh epitomized, and it seemed obvious that Clara and Leigh found pleasure in my parents' company.

Grandma's all-white buffets were so gloriously memorable that I always poked fun at them. She conducted her holiday smorgasbords on Christmas Day, while Aunt Signe held her celebration on Christmas Eve.

In 1941, on Christmas Eve, my grandmother died of a stroke. A chair was left empty at the head of the table in honor of her. That night, after returning home from Aunt Signe's, I saw my father cry for the first time in my life. Pa, who never attended these events, died instantly of heart failure a week later on New Year's Eve.

Aunt Dora, strong and brilliant, went on defining new goals for me. And she continued to add volumes to my Modern Library collection—Dorothy Parker, Thurber, Faulkner, Chekhov. Dora was a celebrated amateur golfer in Minneapolis and won a number of tournaments. She even played with the legendary Patty Berg.

She also had a notable career in the WACs during the latter part of the war when she became one of three executive secretaries (American, English, and French) in India to British Admiral, Lord Louis Mountbatten, the uncle of Prince Charles.

Recently I came across a letter I wrote to Leigh after his beloved Clara died. It read in part: "This is a long overdue letter for so many reasons. My life has been quite an adventure since those golden days of summer at the lake, which I remember so fondly.

"I know you must realize how much you've meant to me all these years. You and Clara have always been my other family, as close to me as my own. So many times I've recalled that you taught me how to drive a car, patiently and kindly. And you taught me how to play poker, you and Clara, and how to appreciate a good cup of coffee, a homemade doughnut, and blueberry pie.

"And, Leigh, you gave me my earliest appreciation of the outdoors—of wilderness, lakes, fishing, and just sitting in a boat with nothing happening and then the great thrill when it did.

"And I'm sure you'll remember you took me into your home, time and time again, as if I were one of yours. And I hope you don't mind my saying that I always felt I was, because I have loved you as much as any son could love a father."

Leigh's response, within a few days, left me reeling. Here, in part, is what he wrote: "I decided that I had better sit right down and thank you for the most wonderful letter that I have ever received. It was sure nice of you to remember all the wonderful times we had together, but don't forget that we enjoyed having you with us, too. Many were the times when Clara and I would say, wouldn't it be wonderful if we could have a son like Curt? Don't think for a minute that I have forgotten about all the fishing trips that we had together and I sure enjoyed your companionship, more than you will ever know."

For the rest of my life, I will be unwrapping all those gifts of love and concern that Clara and Leigh heaped upon me.

ACKNOWLEDGMENTS

In addition to those mentioned in the introduction and the text of this book, a number of good folks are as much family as they are friends, consultants and contributors, cheerleaders and sympathizers:

Anthony D'Elia: *a creative supporter and generous friend*
Ernest H. Holman: *a cousin on my mother's (Holman) side*
Maxine Hyrkas: *who thinks in number, as in money*
Kathryn Larson: *if the truth exists, she can find it*
Pamela McClanahan: *more than my editor, a one-woman show*
David Ogden: *my doctor, who actually makes house calls*
Kenneth and Shirley Olson: *an encore of that happy time*
Lois Severson: *her late mother, Cora, was a great Norse cook*
Elizabeth R. Skok: *my half-niece-in-law, who gets things done*

If moral support means anything, then these communing souls mean everything: Jean Anderson, Lis Brewer, Ann Lindemeyer Burckhardt, John Mack and Sharlyn Carter, Morris Dye, Robert Fetzek, Lee Fowler, Nancy Friday, Harvey and SuEllen Fried, Georgia Hesse, Fred Hill, Mervyn and

Nancy Kaufman, Jerry and Mary King, Gil and Ann Maurer, Dick Moore and Jane Powell, Christine Nord, Sigurd F. Olson, Tom O'Neil, Tracey Pleasant, Geoffrey Precourt, Robin Thoreson, James Villas, Lew Vogler.

Finally, forgive me for failing to acknowledge five of the most deserving people. But you know who you are, don't you?

Curtiss Anderson